MW00996241

PANZER IV

OSPREY
PUBLISHING

PANZ

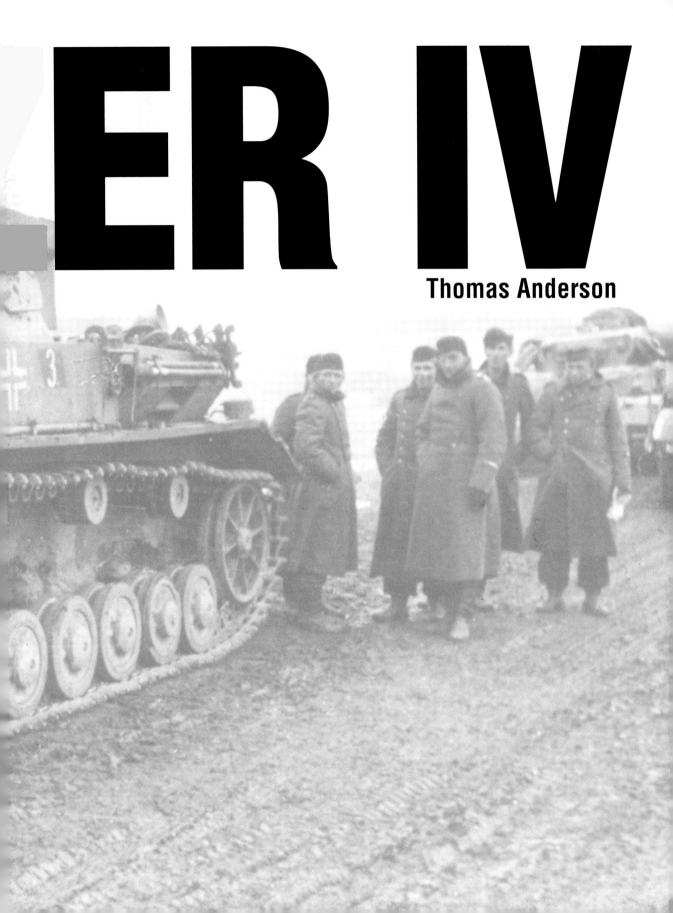

ER IV

Thomas Anderson

Osprey Publishing
c/o Bloomsbury Publishing Plc
Kemp House, Chawley Park, Cumnor Hill, Oxford
OX2 9PH, UK
1385 Broadway, 5th Floor, New York,
NY 10018, USA
E-mail: info@ospreypublishing.com
www.ospreypublishing.com

OSPREY is a trademark of Osprey Publishing Ltd

First published in Great Britain in 2021

ISBN: HB 9781472829689;
eBook 9781472829696;
ePDF 9781472829672;
XML 9781472829702

21 22 23 24 25   10 9 8 7 6 5 4 3 2 1

Conceived and edited by Jasper Spencer-Smith.
Layout: Nigel Pell.
Index by Shaun Barrington.
Produced by Editworks Limited, Bournemouth
BH1 4RT, UK
Printed and bound in India by Replika Press
Private Ltd.

Cover: All images from the collection of
Thomas Anderson.

Osprey Publishing supports the Woodland Trust, the
UK's leading woodland conservation charity.

To find out more about our authors and books visit
www.ospreypublishing.com. Here you will find
extracts, author interviews, details of forthcoming
events and the option to sign up for our newsletter.

MIX
Paper from
responsible sources
FSC® C016779

CONTENTS

Introduction

If the military weapon is a tool of war, then the artisans are the military planners, army commanders and soldiers on the battlefield. A single tank could be deployed as a tactical weapon, whereas a large fast-moving formation (Panzer division) gave military commanders a strategically important advantage.

The development of the tank in Germany was shrouded in secrecy, since the country was still, theoretically, restricted by the Treaty of Versailles. On 11 January 1934, the *Reichswehr* (Germany army) issued a specification for what they called a '*Mittlerer Traktor*' (medium tractor) to various companies including armaments manufacturers. Although designed from the very beginning as a gun-armed tank, the type was somewhat euphemistically known as a *Begleitwagen* (BW – escort vehicle) to maintain secrecy. All pretence stopped on 15 March 1935 when the formation of the *Wehrmacht* (defence force) was announced and Germany began to openly re-arm its military. The BW became known as the *Panzerkampfwagen* (PzKpfw – armoured combat vehicle) IV, and the trials of prototype vehicles built by Rheinmetall-Borsig and Krupp-Grusonwerke continued apace. Eventually, the *Heereswaffenamt* (HWa – army weapons department) decided on the Krupp-Grusonwerke design and accepted it for trials under the designation *Versuchskraftfahrzeug* (VsKfz – experimental motor vehicle) 622. In 1936, the HWa issued a contract to Krupp-Grusonwerke for the production of 750 PzKpfw IV tanks (designated *Sonderkraftfahrzeug* [SdKfz – special purpose vehicle] 161).

The vehicle whose intended role had been 'camouflaged' as an 'escort vehicle' would soon evolve into being the most important tank in the Panzer division, and would remain in front-line service until the fall of Berlin in 1945.

The PzKpfw IV was designed to be cost-effective and straightforward to manufacture in large numbers. The engineering was basic, but the Maybach

Panzer Grenadiers being carried on to their next deployment on a PzKpfw IV Ausf G. The infantry relied on the support of tanks and assault guns to eliminate Red Army machine-gun nests, mortar positions and artillery batteries before and during a battle.

Production of the PzKpfw IV Ausf E began in 1941 and it was the first to have front armour fabricated from 50mm case-hardened steel. The glacis plate was to be reinforced with 30mm armour at a later date.

V12 engine was advanced and the final-drive units were sophisticated but delicate and consequently unreliable. From the very beginning, Krupp-Grusonwerke had decided to position the engine in the rear of the hull, linked by a drive-shaft to the front-mounted transmission.

The seams of the plating forming the hull, superstructure and turret were arc-welded together, where many other nations continued to use the rivet or bolt.

Military planners in most countries, including Germany, considered armour protection to be of incidental importance and most only required proof against 7.92mm *Spitzgeschoss mit Kern* (SmK – armour-piercing bullets) since the tank would always be beyond the range of enemy anti-tank guns. However, already with the second production batch a certain increase of armour thickness was decided.

The running gear – a torsion-bar suspension had been trialled – had eight small-diameter running wheels, mounted in pairs on leaf-sprung bogies. This was a simple system which was designed for reliability and ease of maintenance, but a lack of adequate springing made it uncomfortable for the crew, particularly when operating over uneven terrain.

The lack of a suitable and sufficiently powerful *Panzermotor* (tank engine) caused the HWa to instigate the development of *Hockleistungmotor* (HL – high-performance engine). The company chosen was the highly experienced manufacturer, Maybach-Motorenbau GmbH which had their headquarters and main production facility at Friedrichshafen. The company (assisted by a number of subcontractors) went on to design and manufacture engines and transmissions for most German tanks and a number of half-track vehicles.

The PzKpfw IV was manned by a crew of five; *Panzerführer* (commander), *Fahrer* (driver), *Funker* (wireless operator), *Richtschütze* (gunner) and *Ladeschütze* (loader). Most German tanks were similarly manned throughout the war.

The PzKpfw IV was designed with five access (and escape) hatches which, unlike many Soviet and British tanks, allowed the crew to rapidly evacuate their tank in an emergency. Perhaps this was due to a realistic assessment being made of the time required to fully train a tank crew against that taken to assemble a tank.

At the beginning of the 1930s, the 3.7cm TaK L/45 anti-tank gun was selected as the main weapon for the *Panzerabwehr-Kompanien* (PzAbwKp – tank destroyer companies) and it is not surprising that this weapon was selected to arm the PzKpfw III Ausf A, since this was to be deployed for tank-versus-tank combat.

Since the BW was designed as a support vehicle, it had been decided from the very beginning to mount a 7.5cm *Kampfwagenkanone* (KwK – tank gun) L/24 in the vehicle. Officials at the HWa thought that tank-versus-tank was of secondary importance and decided that the vehicle need only carry high-explosive ammunition and smoke shells.

A PzKpfw IV Ausf E in service with 19.PzDiv on the Russian front in 1941. The tank has been fitted with 30mm spaced armour over the glacis plate to provide the driver and radio operator/ machine gunner with more protection.

When the PzKpfw IV Ausf F (also known as the F/2) mounting a *Langrohr* (lang – long barrelled) 7.5cm KwK 40 L/43 entered service in 1942, German tank crews could fight Soviet T-34 medium and KV-1 heavy tanks on almost equal terms.

A PzKpfw IV Ausf F (lang) in service with 2.SS-PzDiv Das Reich advances through a smoke screen during an exercise. The tank has 30mm add-on amour welded on the front plate and also the glacis.

But experience gained during the invasion of Poland, particularly with regard to the effectiveness of the 7.5cm KwK L/24, caused military planners to deploy the BW for a wider range of tasks. The gun became even more effective when deliveries of a new type of high-explosive ammunition began to arrive for front-line units.

Soon after the launch of *Unternehmen* (Operation) Barbarossa, German military commanders discovered that a PzKpfw III, despite being re-armed with a 5cm KwK L/42 gun, could not defeat the heavily armoured T-34 deployed by the Red Army. The situation did not improve even when the PzKpfw III Ausf J, armed with a high-performance 5cm KwK 39 L/60 gun, entered service in 1942.

To improve the effectiveness of the PzKpfw IV against the latest Soviet armour, including the T-34 medium tank and KV-1 heavy tank, a new type of ammunition was developed: the 7.5cm *Granäte* (Gr) 38 *Hohlladung* (Hl – shaped-charge) shell, deliveries of which began to front-line units at the end of 1941. In mid-1942, the PzKpfw IV Ausf F2 mounting the *Langrohr* (lang – long barrel) 7.5cm KwK L/43 high-performance gun entered service, meaning that the *Panzertruppen* now had a highly-effective main battle tank.

The PzKpfw III and PzKpfw IV were, unlike earlier tanks, fitted with a cupola as standard. The commander would have good all-round visibility through five observation slits, fitted with *Ersatzgläser* (false glass) blocks which were protected from shell splinters by a sliding cover.

This was a quantum leap in German tank development, which now enabled tank forces to attack and defeat every comparable type of enemy tank including the T-34 and the US-built M4 Sherman. But, nevertheless, German tank forces were numerically inferior, which meant they had to improve or adopt better tactics, even improvise, on the battlefield.

To establish their clear superiority on the battlefield, military planners in Germany ordered the design and development of two superior types: the PzKpfw V Panther medium tank and the PzKpfw VI Tiger Ausf E heavy tank.

But these would never be produced in sufficient quantities, since the German armaments industry did not (and perhaps never would) have the capacity or sufficient materials to match the industrial capabilities of the USA and the Soviet Union.

Another factor was that production of the PzKpfw IV could not be stopped in favour of the new of the types – the loss of production would have caused the situation for German forces fighting on at the Eastern Front to become even more critical. For this reason, the original *Begleitwagen* version would remain in production until the end of the war.

This book explains the origins, development and production of the PzKpfw IV, but will not be a detailed 'nuts and bolts' history, since this has been more than adequately covered by Spielberger and Thomas Jentz.

Of greater importance is how the PzKpfw IV was distributed within German training and front-line units and its deployment on all battlefronts. A number of after-action reports have been included in the text which provide a glimpse of what it was like to fight a battle from a PzKpfw IV.

The tables of organization were compiled by carefully examining wartime documents and all symbols shown are those as used by the German military. The tables varied over the course of time according to changes to the *Kriegsstärkenachweisung* (KStN – tables of organization) which authorized the type of equipment and the number that should be supplied, but the German armaments industry was never able to deliver the required quantities. The problem was further exacerbated as significant combat losses depleted the number of tanks held in reserve. Consequently, regimental commanders were forced to improvise by distributing any available tanks equally among units, or to form *Kampfgruppen* (battle groups) or *Ersatz-Abteilungen* (mixed battalions).

A fine example is the May 1940 order of battle: The newly introduced *mittlere Panzerkompanie* (m PzKp – medium tank company) to KStN 1175

In January 1941, 3.PzDiv was, like many others, involved in extensive field manoeuvres in preparation for *Unternehmen Barbarossa*. The PzKpfw IV Ausf D has a non-standard one-digit identifier on the turret, but this would be changed to three-digits before the launch of the invasion of the Soviet Union on June 1941.

(Sd) authorized each company to have a complement of 14 PzKpfw IV; at that time a standard Panzer division would have four such companies, and were often referred to as *schwere Kompanien* (s Kp – heavy companies). But the planned strength could not be implemented. For example, at the beginning of *Fall Gelb* (Case Yellow), 4.PzDiv had only 24 PzKpfw IV in its inventory, a sharp contrast to the officially authorized number of 56.

Any errors in the tables, which may contradict some of those reproduced in other works, are due to a general vagueness found in many official documents produced during the war.

Importantly, the term main battle tank (MBT) was first adopted in the 1960s, when a new type of medium tank armed with a high-performance gun entered service, a good example being the German-designed and built Leopard.

The PzKpfw IV Ausf H, armed with a 7.5cm KwK L/48, was considered a stop gap solution until the PzKpfw V Panther medium tank, armed with 7.5cm KwK 42 L/70, entered service.

Finally, in 1943 production of the *Sturmgeschütz* III, armed with a 7.5cm *Sturmkanone* (StuK – assault gun) 40 L/48, became of equal importance; a fact that must never be forgotten.

Thomas Anderson
November 2020

In response to the effective anti-tank rifles in service with the Red Army, military planners decided, in mid-1943, that *Panzerschürzen* (tank skirts) were to be fitted on German tanks and *Sturmgeschütz* (StuG – assault guns). The plates would be fitted at the factory, but kits would also be sent to front-line workshops to be fitted on vehicles in service. Tank No.832 is a PzKpfw IV Ausf G and is one of those fitted with *Nebelkurze* (smoke candle discharger) on the turret.

Origins 1

The *Reichswehr* (German army) was formed in 1921 and incorporated, along with air and naval forces, into the *Deutsche Wehrmacht* (defence force) on 16 March 1935. The new 'defensive' force was to be equipped with the most modern weapons which were to be deployed using new, somewhat, revolutionary tactics. The transformation had been carried out in complete secrecy and in defiance of the conditions accepted by Germany on signing the Treaty of Versailles.

Production of 150 *Landwirtschaftlichter-Ackerschlepper* (LaS – agricultural farm tractor) began at Henschel in July 1934. The vehicle entered service with the *Wehrmacht* and was originally designated *Panzerkampfwagen (Maschinengewehr) Ausführung* A (PzKw [MG] Ausf A – armoured fighting vehicle [machine gun] model A), but this was changed to PzKw I (MG) Ausf B in 1935 and later listed as the *Sonderkraftfahrzeug* (SdKfz – special purpose vehicle) 101. The light tank was originally armed with two license-built 7.7mm Vickers water-cooled machine guns, but these were replaced by two 7.92mm *Machinengewehr* 13 of German origin. The first Panzer divisions to be established were equipped with the type where it was used to train thousands of *Panzertruppen* (armoured troops).

In 1932, the *Reichswehr* initiated a series of military manoeuvres to assess the type of armoured vehicles required and how they should be effectively deployed on a battlefield. But due to treaty restrictions only a few armoured vehicles were available, and most were dummy vehicles fabricated from wood and canvas.

A report, *Taktik der Kampfwagen* (tactics of combat vehicles), was subsequently published by *Waffenprüfämter Inspektion* 6:

> 2.) The armoured combat vehicle is to be considered purely as an attack weapon and must only be deployed to overcome enemy resistance at focal points on the

The *Grosstraktor* (large tractor) II was built by Rheinmetall-Borsig to a secret order issued by the *Heereswaffenamt* (army weapons department) in 1929. The large frame-type aerial, mounted on the engine compartment decking, indicates that the vehicle has been fitted with radio equipment.

battlefield. Here, they temporarily become the main asset in the attack.

3.) Since the type is extremely mobile and heavily armed, each unit will be allocated a specific target. Their attack must not be compromised by slower vehicles.

5.) Any commitment in less than battalion strength must be rejected. Consideration must be given to the enemy deploying anti-tank devices and guns which can delay or hinder an assault by a tank company even during a surprise attack.

17.) It is generally considered necessary for the staff section of a tank battalion to have a light tank platoon. This is of great importance for reconnaissance duties and for maintaining communications with the companies and other units.

By 1932 a new medium tank type had been developed, the *Neubaufahrzeug* (NbFz – new build vehicle). The design was typical of a that featured on a number of types built by various nations during the inter-war period: a turret mounting the main weapon and an auxiliary machine-gun armed turret.

Although the manoeuvres were on a small scale, they did provide commanders with some knowledge as to how the *Kampfwagen* (Kw – armoured fighting vehicle [tank]) could be deployed for a rapid, concentrated and surprise attack – the *Blitzkrieg* (lightning war) successfully employed by German forces on many fronts in the opening years of World War II.

But how could the gathered information be used in reality and was there sufficient capacity in the German armaments industry to build and maintain a supply of armoured vehicles. Interestingly, the report does not contain any technical comment with regard to armament or mechanical performance and reliability.

Left: A dummy tank constructed from wood and canvas has been fitted on the chassis of a BMW 'Dixie' – a license-built Austin 7 – passenger car.

Below: A column of dummy armoured vehicles from a *Panzertruppen* training unit. The type was built from thin metal sheet and utilized the chassis of an Adler passenger car.

The order to develop the first tank was issued by the *Reichswehr* in 1928 and, due to treaty restrictions, was given the code name *Grosstraktor* (large tractor). The first tanks produced were constructed from non-armoured steel plates and were armed with a 7.5cm short-barrelled gun: possibly experience gained during World War I indicated that this was the most effective weapon for fighting soft targets, including entrenched infantry and also artillery positions, at very close range. It is possible that the type was the forerunner of the *Begleitwagen* (BW – escort vehicle).

The experience gained after trials of the *Grosstraktor* was somewhat confused and it must be assumed that series production was never planned. This suggests that the *Reichswehr* viewed the type as only an experimental vehicle. Another type also under development was the 3.7cm-armed tank; code named the *Kleintraktor* (light tractor).

The last three of five NbFz were fabricated from armoured steel plate. Crews received gunnery training at Putlos before the tanks were sent to Norway in April 1940 as part of *Panzerabteilung zür besonderen Verfügung* (PzAbt [zbV] – tank battalion for special duties) 40.

In 1928 a British company, Vickers-Armstrong, produced a light tank as a private venture: the Vickers 6-ton (Vickers Mark E) tank was simple and cost-effective to construct and was built in two versions: Type A, with two turrets each mounting a .303in Vickers water-cooled machine gun; Type B with a two-man turret mounting an Ordnance Quick-Firing (QF) 3-pounder gun and a Vickers water-cooled machine gun. Although the Mark E was not purchased for the British Army, the government granted the manufacturer permission to export the tank to other nations.

More than ten foreign armies procured the Vickers 6-ton tank, including the Soviet Union which also purchased a production license. By 1930 the Russians, using the Mark E as a pattern, had completed the design and development of their own variant; the T-26. This was the first tank to be mass produced and more than 10,000 had been completed when production ended in 1941.

Right: One of the three NbFz, which had been at Putlos, at sea on a cargo ship for delivery Norway in 1940 as part of PzAbt (vbZ) 40.

Below: *Unternehmen* Weserübung was launched on *Wesertag* (Weser Day) – 9 April 1940 – by an invasion of Denmark and would end on 10 June 1940 after Norway had been occupied. After the operation the three NbFz deployed were, subsequently, used only for training purposes.

Most certainly German military planners would have been aware of the large number of tanks entering Red Army service. This possibly induced them to consider that the development of the tank should be given greater importance in Germany.

In 1932 the *Heereswaffenamt* (HWa – army weapons department) issued the specification for a new type of tank; designated *mittlerer Traktor oder Grosstraktor* (*Neubau*) (medium or large tractor [new build]) which, in some respects, appeared to be a modification of the original *Grosstraktor* design, being fitted with a main turret and two separate turrets each mounting a *Maschinengewehr* (MG – machine gun). The vehicle weighed 15,241kg and was powered by a 250hp BMW IV six-cylinder liquid-cooled petrol engine originally produced for use in aircraft. Subsequently, WaPrüf 6 issued development contracts to two companies; Rheinmetall-Borsig was to produce a complete vehicle, while Krupp was only to design and build an alternative turret. The type received the designation *Neubaufahrzeug* (NbFz – new vehicle).

In 1933 the final design emerged. Not untypical for this era it was a multi-turreted tank: the main turret mounted a 7.5cm KwK L/24 gun firing high-explosive ammunition and a 3.7cm KwK 36 L/45 for combat against armoured

The few *Grosstraktor* (large tractor) built were used as trials vehicles and then to train the first crews selected for the future tank army. Trials began at the end of the 1929 and to maintain secrecy and, since Germany was still restricted by the Treaty of Versailles, much of this work was done in Kazan in the Soviet Union.

targets. For self-defence, the vehicle was fitted with a further two turrets each armed with a 7.92mm MG 13/34 machine gun. The first prototype, completed in 1934, was fabricated from mild-steel sheet; a second vehicle was completed, using the same non-armour material, in 1935. Subsequently, WaPrüf 6 issued contracts for three to be produced, using steel armour plate, and delivered ready for a series of trials.

Only the five NbFz prototypes were completed and, since there is little further information available, it can be assumed that series production was never intended.

Apparently, a number of problems were encountered during the trials: the BMW engine took up too much space in the hull and it did not provide sufficient torque at low rpm; very unfavourable for an armoured vehicle. Another problem was that the tracks frequently jumped off the sprockets, but this was investigated by the constructor and traced to the rear drive unit.

Although the well-armed *Neubaufahrzeug* was designed to perform two roles, the *Heereswaffenamt* decided in 1936 to initiate the development of two different battle tanks.

Eastern Front 1941: German infantry supported by PzKpfw IV from 6.PzDiv, part of *Heeresgruppe Nord* (Army Group North), advance towards the city of Leningrad.

1936–1938
The *Panzertruppe*
2

In 1934 a number of fundamental changes took place; the HWa was completely reorganized as officials were made aware of how the tank would be deployed in any future conflict. The first combat tank to be developed, the *Grosstraktor* was to be fitted with a 7.5cm KwK L/24 gun, while the NbFz was specifically designed as a universal 'breakthrough' tank.

No records exist detailing why the concept of a universal tank was abandoned, but the HWa did give priority to the design of specialist tanks, while at the same time progressing the development of smaller and cheaper types; the LaS (PzKpfw I) and the LaS 100 (PzKpfw II). [Note: It is not clear to what extent or even if the NbFz was ever intended to be a 'multi-purpose tank'.]

General Oswald Lutz and, at that time *Oberstleutnant* Heinz Guderian – he had previously been involved in the development of the *Neubaufahrzeug* – quickly adapted their proposed tactics for when the new types entered service.

The proven 3.7cm KwK 36 L/45 and a 7.5cm KwK L/24, which had been used to arm the *Neubaufahrzeug*, were selected as the main weapons for two different armoured types which were under development. Since the *Deutsche Reich* was still under special (if somewhat ineffective) observation, each new development was given a code name and work was carried out in strict secrecy.

In April 1935, Adolf Hitler defiantly repudiated the limitations set out in the Treaty of Versailles and continued with his dream of building an all-conquering *Wehrmacht*.

At the same as Hitler was withdrawing from the treaty, HWa officials issued contracts for the development of the new types.

The chassis No.80110 identifies this as one of the first PzKpfw IV Ausf A to be built. The vehicle is fitted with a track link carrier and the new type of ball mounting for the *Maschinengewehr* (MG – machine gun) 34 introduced, which was used on the PzKpfw IV Ausf D.

A wooden mock-up of the superstructure for a *Begleitwagen* (BW – escort tank) II in the experimental workshop at Krupp-Grusonwerke. Note the open access hatch for the transmission.

The first was to be known as a *Zugführerwagen* (ZW – platoon commander's vehicle) which, as the name suggests, was built to lead an attack. The type was to be armed with a 3.7cm KwK L/45; a powerful anti-tank weapon, which had also been issued to front-line anti-tank gun units in the newly formed Wehrmacht. Since the ZW was built to directly confront enemy positions, the vehicle was to have substantial front armour. A contract for the development of the vehicle was issued to Daimler-Benz; the company went on to design and manufacture the PzKpfw III.

The second was known as a *Begleitwagen* (BW – escort vehicle) which was to monitor the battlefield and provide supporting fire when required. The BW was armed with a 7.5cm KwK L/24 primarily to knock out enemy anti-tank and gun artillery positions with high-explosive ammunition, but the weapon could also fire armour-piercing and smoke shells. The BW would eventually be designated as the *Sonderkraftfahrzeug* (SdKfz – special purpose vehicle) 161 or PzKpfw IV.

Original documentation on the development, including detailed specification sheets, of the ZW and BW could not be found. But again, as with the NbFz, both types were scrutinized by military officials who then decided to order the design of a completely new vehicle.

Experience gained from trials with the *Grosstraktor*, where the tracks were frequently thrown off the sprockets, caused engineers to re-think the design. and, as a result, the hull. After discovering the problem was not caused by the sprocket, but by the rear-mounted final-drive unit, the transmission system was completely redesigned and positioned in the front of the hull as in the LaS and LaS 100.

Two manufacturers were contracted to design and produce the different types, but both were to have the same mechanical layout – transmission at the front and engine in the rear – which became standard practice on all

Above: Rheinmetall-Borsig used the suspension from the earlier NbFz for their BW prototype and also retained rear-wheel drive, whereas Krupp-Grusonwerke decided to use six-wheel running gear with torsion-bar suspension and re-positioned the transmission at the front of the hull.

Left: The Rheinmetal-Borsig prototype featured a large longitudinal deflector plate which was positioned under the return rollers to prevent mud falling from the tracks and clogging the running gear.

A Maybach HL 120 TRM in the workshop: The V12-cylinder water-cooled petrol engine which developed 300hp; the acronym HL is for *Hockleistungsmotor* (high-performance engine) and TRM is for *Trockensumpfschmierung mit Schnappermagnet* (dry sump lubrication; magneto ignition).

German tanks. Also both companies were ordered to utilize interchangeable components including the tracks, running wheels and the engine.

High-performance Engines

Up until 1930, only a small number of engines with sufficient performance were available. The *Grosstraktor* and the *Neubaufahrzeug* were both fitted with a BMW engine, a solution far from ideal. The LaS 100 was powered by 3,300cc Krupp M305 six-cylinder horizontally opposed (Boxer) air-cooled petrol engine, as used in their Kfz 69 light truck known as the 'Protze'.

In 1935 Maybach Motorenbau was selected by the HWa as the sole designer of *Panzermotoren* (P – tank engines) for the German army. The first was the NL 38 TR, a 3,790cc six-cylinder water-cooled *Normalleistung* (NL – normal performance) petrol engine with *Trockensumpfschmierung* (TR – dry sump lubrication) which was used to power the PzKpfw I Ausf B. The company then designed a 6,190cc six-cylinder water-cooled *Hochleistungmotor* (HL – high performance) petrol engine for the PzKpfw II (HL 62 TR). The search for more power resulted in a compact 10,840cc V12-cylinder water-cooled petrol engine (HL108TR) which was selected to power the PzKpfw III and the first version of the PzKpfw IV. By the end of the war, Maybach had designed a 23,880cc V12-cylinder engine to power the PzKpfw VI Ausf B, Tiger II heavy tank.

Such was the demand for tank engines that Maybach was forced to outsource a significant part of production to other companies which included Norddeutsche Motorenbau in Berlin.

Birth of the BW

Two companies, Rheinmetall-Borsig and Krupp-Grusonwerke, were both contracted to design a support tank and produce prototype vehicles for development trials.

Rheinmetall-Borsig delivered their version at the end of 1935 which was assembled using a number of components – wheel bogies, suspension and running gear – from the *Neubaufahrzeug*, but powered by a Maybach HL108TR water-cooled petrol engine. Initially the company had planned to fit their version with two turrets, but these were still under development and the trials vehicles were delivered fitted a corresponding amount of weight. Almost as soon as the trials began, the HWa decided that the vehicle was unsuitable and cancelled all future work.

In 1936, Krupp had completed their design work and delivered two prototypes. The hull was fabricated from welded steel armour plate and, to equalize weight distribution, the transmission (gearbox and final drive) was mounted in the front and the engine in the rear. This became standard practice for all future German tanks.

The running gear on the Krupp version had eight small double running wheels on each side and was fitted with a turret mounting a 7.5cm KwK L/24; the manufacturer never intended to fit a secondary turret.

Krupp-Grusonwerke delivered, without a turret, the prototype of an alternative version, the BW II Kp. The vehicle utilized the BW I hull, mechanical layout and HL 100 TR engine, but was fitted with torsion-bar suspension and six large diameter running wheels.

Information found in contemporary documents indicates that trials with the torsion-bar suspension were disappointing, causing the company to abandon any future development work.

PzKpfw IV Ausf A

The HWa issued the order for a first production series in December 1936, but before this commenced the design was refined, and virtually all the components were reworked. The first series received the designation

Above: A production PzKpfw IV Ausf C: As on the Ausf B, the front plate on the superstructure is now slightly angled and there is no ball-mounted machine gun. The vehicle has the 1939-type solid white cross; a rhomboid-shaped plate.

Right: The PzKpfw IV Ausf A was fitted a rudimentary cupola which gave only limited armour protection for the commander. The narrow vision slits would also have limited his view of the battlefield.

1./BW, and this would continue to be used by the armaments industry throughout the war: the HWa designated it as the PzKpfw IV Ausf A with the identifier *Sonderkraftfahrzeug* (SdKfz – special purpose vehicle) 161.

Production began in June 1936 at the Krupp-Grusonwerke factory in Magdeburg and ended in November 1937 after a total of 35 had left the assembly lines.

The front of the vehicle was protected 14.5mm-thick armour while that on the turret was 20mm, but this only provided protection against infantry armour-piercing ammunition and shell fragments. Military planners considered this to be adequate since the BW would not be deployed at the spearhead of an attack.

The main gun, a 7.5cm KwK L/24, was mounted in a rotatable turret with a coaxial *Maschinengewehr* (MG – machine gun) 34. A second MG 34, for self-defence, was mounted in the hull and fired by the wireless operator; the coaxial MG could be dismounted and fired through the gun ports in the rear of the turret. The same weapon could also be mounted for anti-aircraft defence.

The PzKpfw IV Ausf A carried a crew of five; commander, gunner, loader, wireless operator/MG gunner and driver. All German tanks would be crewed like this in the future.

The PzKpfw I Ausf A was initially equipped with a *Funkgerät* (FuG – radio device) 6; a 20W Sender (S – transmitter) 'c' and a UHF (ultra-high frequency) *Empfänger* (E – receiver) 'c1'. The transmitter had a range of 3km to 6km (voice) and up to 8km (Morse), but for an unknown reason this radio was soon replaced. It was then equipped with the FuG 5 type; a 10W S 'c' transmitter and an *Empfänger* 'e' which had a significantly reduced range of 2km to 4km (voice). When the PzKpfw IV Ausf B entered production, the wireless equipment was improved by fitting a second *Empfänger* 'e' (FuG 2 radio).

PzKpfw IV Ausf A		PzKpfw IV Ausf B	
Weight:	18,290kg	Weight:	18,690kg
Engine:	Maybach HL100 TR	Engine:	Maybach HL120 TR
Performance:	250hp	Performance:	265hp
Speed (maximum):	32.4kph	Speed (maximum):	42kph
Range (road):	210km	Range (road):	210km
Range (cross country):	130km	Range (cross country):	130km
Trench crossing:	2.3m	Trench crossing:	2.3m
Fording depth:	80cm	Fording depth:	80cm
Ground clearance:	40cm	Ground clearance:	40cm

A pre-production PzKpfw IV Ausf D undergoing suspension and running gear trials. The prototype BW built by Krupp-Grusonwerke had six-wheel torsion bar suspension, but it proved to be too fragile. Consequently, the company designed a new type featuring eight (double) wheels mounted on four leaf-sprung bogeys.

As production of the Ausf A continued, officials at the HWa decided to issue a contract for the 2./BW (PzKpfw IV Ausf B), an almost complete redesign for which almost all components were examined and improved where necessary. One major requirement was that the front armour must be increased from 14.5mm to 30mm.

7.5cm KwK L/24

The gun had a relatively short barrel and did not need to be fitted with a counterweight. In 1935, German military planners were confident that the gun would be effective against all known French tanks.

On 30 October 1935, a *Waffenamt* (ordnance office) issued a report:

> The 7.5cm *Kampfwagenkanone* has a calibre length of L/24 and a muzzle velocity of 430mps. When firing the 7.5cm Panzergranate [7.5cm KGr rot Pz] 43mm of armour was penetrated at an angle of 60 degrees which makes it eminently suitable for defeating the new French tank types [these had 40mm armour]. However, these are theoretical considerations which will have to be proven by practical trials at Putlos; the low muzzle velocity results in a curved trajectory which will seriously affect accuracy. Despite this, we expect the BW to defeat all types of French tanks with the exception of the Char 2C super heavy tank.

Left: A PzKpfw IV Ausf B from 3.PzDiv on the training grounds at its home garrison in Zossen. The advantage of using front drive is evident; the drive sprocket is relatively clear – any build-up of mud could throw a track.

Below: Early 1940, a PzKpfw IV Ausf B deployed for a live-firing exercise as part of the preparations being made for the *Blitzkrieg* (lightning attack) across northern Europe in May. The tank can be identified as being from 2.PzDiv, by two white dots painted to the side of the white outline-type cross.

It is thought than an increased muzzle velocity of approximately 650mps should make it possible to defeat a Char 2C. But such an increase in performance would require construction of a new tank to mount such a gun, which – assuming it had minimal 20mm armour – would have an operational weight of 30,480kg. But only recently, the Commander-in-Chief of the army stated that he was against such a solution.

Established at Würzburg in 1935, PzRgt 4 as part of 2.PzDiv was issued with the PzKpfw IV Ausf A in late 1937. Some months after the annexation of Austria, on 14 March 1938, the division was transferred to its new garrison in Vienna.

The above note appears to contradict the proposed deployment of the BW as a support tank. But it does show that the German military was completely aware of the heavily armoured French tanks long before the outbreak of the war.

Also, it is interesting to note that Somua S-35 cavalry tank was not individually recognized and, even more mysterious, the Char B1 bis (60mm armour) has not received a mention. The suggestion to mount a more powerful gun is interesting, since the issue was reconsidered in 1941.

The 7.5cm KwK fired the following ammunition:

The 7.5cm GrPatr 34 was a conventional high-explosive shell fitted with a standard *kleiner Aufschlagzünder* (kl AZ – small impact fuse) 23 and was used to attack entrenched infantry – shrapnel had a lethal effect – or those concealed in buildings. Care had to be taken when firing it at a low angle, especially over hard terrain, since the round could ricochet and miss the target. The shell when fitted with a delay fuse was highly effective for attacking reinforced emplacements, shelters and buildings.

The 7.5cm KGr rot Pz, occasionally referred to as PzGr Patr KwK, was used for tank-versus-tank combat. A detonation fuse was fitted in the base of the shell which also had a had a tracer with two-second burn time to allow a gunner to observe the trajectory.

The PzKpfw IV Ausf B and Ausf C were built with thicker front armour and a more powerful Maybach engine. But for an unknown reason the ball-mounted machine gun was replaced by a pistol port.

7.5cm KwK

Calibre:	7.5cm
Length of gun barrel:	1766.5mm (L/24)
Max firing range:	6500m
V° GrPatr 34:	420m/sec
V° KGr rot Pz:	385m/sec
Side traverse:	360°
Elevation range:	-10° to + 20°
Rate of fire:	10–20rpm
Weight:	490kg

Elements of PzRgt 1 of (1.PzDiv) on the training grounds at their home garrison, in 1938. The regiment is mainly equipped (like many others) with PzKpfw I and PzKpfw II, since very few PzKpfw III and IV were available. The lead tank in the second column from the left is a PzKpfw IV Ausf B.

14 March 1938: A column of PzKpfw IV Ausf A from PzRgt 4 (2.PzDiv), parade through Vienna as part of the force that peacefully annexed Austria.

The 7.5cm NbGrPatr was the standard smoke shell which could, depending on weather conditions, produce cloud of smoke some 15m to 20m in diameter. Supply was carefully controlled and it was only used when conditions were suitable or in a dire emergency.

During production of the first series (1./BW or PzKpfw IV Ausf A) the HWa began to modify its requirements which included a demand for the front armour to be proof against 20mm anti-tank weapons.

As Krupp-Grusonwerke made preparations to begin production of the next batch it also decided to implement a number of improvements:

- The shape of the hull was altered since the width of the *Bugpanzer* (bow plate) was reduced. The armour was increased to 30mm.
- The armour on the front of the turret was increased to 30mm.
- The design of the *Panzerführer-Kuppel* (commander's cupola) was improved to give much better protection.

Also, the front of the superstructure was straightened and, somewhat confusingly, the hull-mounted MG was deleted and replaced with a pistol port. Another improvement was to replace the driver's visor with an easier to operate sliding type.

These and other modifications resulted in the weight of the vehicle increasing from 18,695kg to 19,102kg.

To compensate for this, it was decided to fit a more powerful 11,870cc Maybach HL120TR engine which required a six-speed Zahnradfabrik (ZF) SSG 76 gearbox to be fitted in place of the original five-speed SFG 75.

Between May and October 1938, production of the 2./BW (PzKpfw IV Ausf B) was a total of 42. A wartime document from Krupp-Grusonwerke notes that some 130 individual companies were subcontracted to assist in the production of the PzKpfw IV Ausf B.

In July 1938, *Inspektion* 6 reported to *Allgemeines Heeresamt*, (AHA – general army department) and issued a detailed list of the total number of tanks ordered: 2,155 PzKpfw III (3.7cm) and 640 PzKpfw IV (7.5cm). But no delivery dates were given. The order shown for the PzKpfw IV was not completed until July 1941.

Organizational Issues

The organizational structure for all light and medium Panzer companies was, in principle, detailed by the valid KStN. Unfortunately, many of the early KStN

A PzKpfw IV Ausf B positioned on a *Brückengerät* 'B' bridging section carried on pontoons during one of the many exercises held in preparation for *Unternehmen* Barbarossa.

A column of PzKpfw IV Ausf B from an unknown unit parade through Vienna.

PzKpfw IV Production:

1937		Total Stock
November	2	2
December	4	6
1938		
January	4	10
February	5	15
March	5	20
April	5	25
May	12	37
June	12	49
July	7	56
August	7	63
September	7	70
October	7	77
November	12	89
December	14	103

Above: Three PzKpfw IV Ausf C parked in front of a telegraph office. Note the coaxial machine gun 34 is now fitted with an armoured sleeve.

Left: A PzKpfw IV Ausf A during the occupation of Czechoslovakia. Note the distinctve sloped bow plate and the early type of cupola.

A column of PzKpfw IV Ausf B photographed at their garrison before the war. The tank carries no markings: even the vehicle number plate holder is empty.

are not available, since orders were issued for them to be destroyed when a newer version was issued.

But war diaries kept by a number of tank divisions have been discovered. A document from 1938 details the structure of a *Panzerabteilung* (PzAbt – tank battalion) which had three *leichter Panzerkompanien* (le PzKp – light tank companies) in accordance to KStN 1171; and a light tank company in accordance to KStN 1175. This indicates that the latter was the relevant organizational structure for the PzKpfw IV. But due to the limited availability of tanks, the document indicates that there were only three *Geschützkampfwagen* (gun tanks [PzKpfw IV]); the rest of the equipment consisted of PzKpfw I, PzKpfw II and PzKpfw III. Another type listed was a variant of the PzKpfw I Ausf B fitted with extensive radio equipment to serve as a *Panzerbefehlswagen* (PzBefWg – commander's tank).

It should be noted that the equipment actually supplied to the Panzer divisions invariably deviated from those stated in a KStN: many treated the documents as an 'ideal solution'. Military planners for a long time sought to equip a 'PzKpfw IV *Kompanie*' with 14 of the type.

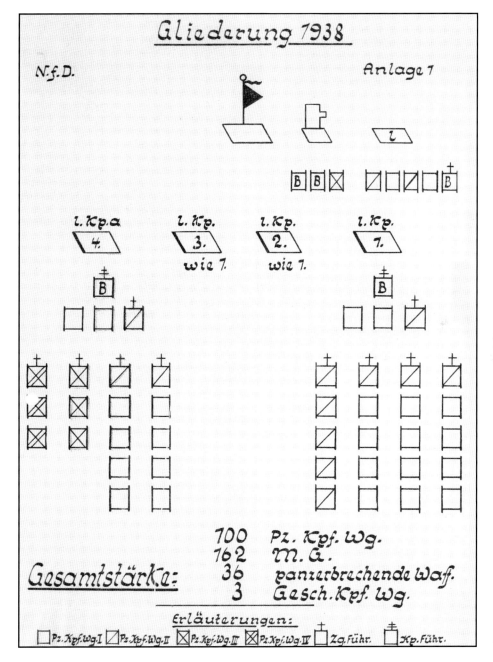

Kriegstärkenachweissung (KStN - organizational structure) published in 1938 for a standard *Panzerabteilung* (PzAbt – tank battalion).

The interior of a PzKpfw IV Ausf A. The seat for the commander is at the rear of the turret with that for the gunner in front. The glass vision blocks in the cupola are clearly visible.

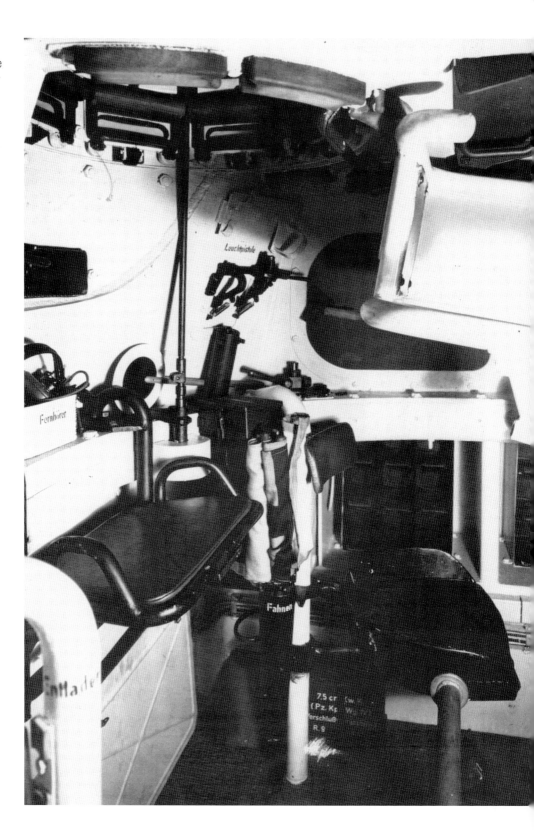

Ersatzgläser

7.5cm
MG34

Above: The compact breech assembly of a 7.5cm KwK L/24 mounted in a PzKpfw IV. Note the (empty) mounting for the coaxial *Machinengewehr* (MG – machine gun) 34.

Left: The *Turmzielfernrohr* (TZF – turret sighting telescope), above which is the gun travelling lock. A spare barrel for the machine gun was stored to the left of the telescope. The gun elevation and traversing controls were positioned under the breech assembly.

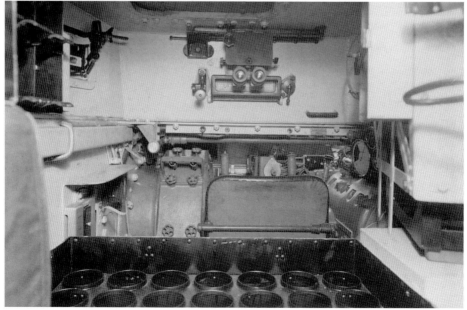

Above: The radio operator's position in a PzKpfw IV Ausf B. The radio equipment is stowed in racks at the left. Note the vision device and the locking handle for the pistol port.

Right: The driver's position. A total of 28 rounds of 7.5cm ammunition was carried inside a PzKpfw IV Ausf A, and all was stowed in a rack positioned behind the driver.

Far right: The radio operator's seat in a PzKpfw IV Ausf A.

1939 – *Fall Weiss*

In early 1937, WaPrüf 6 informed Krupp-Grusonwerke that they had made a decision which would also prove to have far-reaching implications. They had decided to simplify production; the BW and ZW were to be built on a standardized chassis which incorporated the design features from the latest version of the ZW (PzKpfw III Ausf E). The chassis selected was from the fourth production batch (4./ZW) which had been designed with six-wheel running gear mounted on torsion-bar suspension to improve mobility. This was further improved by fitting the type with a Maybach Variorex SGR 328 ten-speed semi-automatic gearbox driven by a Maybach HL 120 TRM engine.

The decision also meant that production of the BW at Krupp-Grusonwerke was to end after an order for 42 PzKpfw IV Ausf B had been completed.

Although work to re-engineer the BW turret so that it could be fitted on a PzKpfw III Ausf E chassis was at an advanced stage, the lack of capacity (and resources) in the German armaments industry would intervene. Also, the work required to adapt the assembly lines at Krupp-Grusonwerke to build the ZW chassis would have resulted in a distinct gap in the production of the PzKpfw IV, which would have spelled disaster for the *Panzerwaffe*. As a result, it was decided that the manufacturer would continue producing the PzKpfw IV; subsequently an order was issued for a third batch of BW tanks in October 1937. A shortage of time allowed for only few improvements to be made, the most noticeable of which was the fitting of an armoured sleeve over the barrrel of the turret MG. The type was also fitted with a more powerful Maybach HL 120 TRM: HL – *Hockleitungmotor* (high-performance engine); TRM – *Trockensumpfschmierung mit Schnappermagnet* (dry sump lubrication with magneto ignition). A total of 140 PzKpfw IV Ausf C were produced between October 1938 and August 1939.

Up until 1940, 2.PzDiv used a distinctive identifier by having two white dots stencilled on the front, the sides and rear of its vehicles. This PzKpfw IV Ausf C also has a white rhomboid on the bow plate denoting that it is from 5.*Kompanie* (Kp – company).

Fall Weiss (Case White)

In the final stages of preparation for *Fall Weiss* (Case White), the invasion of Poland, seven standard Panzer divisions and four *leichte Divisionen* (leDiv – light divisions) were mobilized and another three battalions placed on stand-by at *Heerestruppen* (army) level.

At that the time standard Panzer divisions were not uniformly formed, being issued with a varying number of *Panzerabteilungen* (PzAbtn – tank battalions): for example 3.PzDiv had five battalions; 1.PzDiv, 2.PzDiv, 4.PzDiv and 5.PzDiv had four battalions; 1.leDiv had three battalions; PzDiv Kempf and 10.PzDiv each had two battalions.

The long-term plan was to provide each *Panzerabteilung* (PzAbt – tank battalion) with two *leichte Panzerkompanie* (le PzKp - light tank company) in accordance to KStN 1171) equipped with 14 PzKpfw III, and a *mittlere Panzerkompanie* (m PzKp – medium tank company) in accordance to KStN 1175 equipped with 14 PzKpfw IV. Both KStN note that there was also a *leichte Panzerzug* (light tank platoon) equipped with five PzKpfw II.

By the summer of 1939, the number of companies in each battalion had been effectively reduced to three and due to a lack of PzKpfw III military

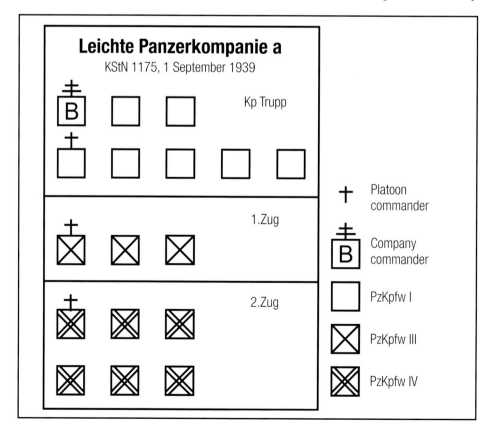

The formation for a light tank company in 1939.

planners were forced to integrate the few available together with PzKpfw IV as a light company PzKp in accordance with KStN 1175.

The four light divisions established in the years before the war were formed with differing structures since it had originally been planned to equip all with only light tanks. In combat, the medium tanks of the Panzer division would be deployed to break through the enemy lines, whereas the light division was deployed for reconnaissance operations, and often behind the enemy lines. On many occasions, due to their high speed and mobility, they were called on to close-off any gap in the frontline or even to capture important terrain.

Troops inspect a PzKpfw IV Ausf B which has been hit by some three 37mm rounds fired by Polish anti-tank gunners. One has hit the gun housing, another the armoured lip which protected the turret ring and a third the front plate on the superstructure.

By 1 September 1939 the German army attacked with the following tank strength

Tank strength as of 1 Sept 1939, *Fall Weiss*, invasion of Poland

Type	Number
PzKpfw I	1026
PzKpfw II	1151
PzKpfw 35(t)	164
PzKpfw 3 (t)	57
PzKpfw III	87
PzKpfw IV	194
PzBefWg	177
StuG	0

Above: Mechanics remove a damaged Maybach HL 120 TRM engine from a PzKpfw IV with a block and tackle suspended from a simple wooden tripod.

Right: Engineers have removed the drive sprocket from this PzKPfw IV Ausf A so that the drive unit can be examined. The unit contained an assembly of planetary and epicyclic gears which made it almost impossible to repair in the field.

Even before the Polish campaign their intended usage was apparently being questioned, and the decision was made to convert all light divisions into regular Panzer divisions.

The conversion was successfully implemented with 1.leDiv; the only light division to be equipped with PzKpfw IV tanks for remaining three le PzKp. The other six le PzKp had their PzKpfw III replaced by PzKpfw 35(t). In contrast, 2.leDiv and 4.leDiv were issued with PzKpfw I and PzKpfw II, whereas 3.leDiv was equipped with PzKpfw II and PzKpfw 38(t).

In Action

As one of the first units to be issued with PzKpfw IV, 1./PzRgt 1 was equipped with the type for the invasion of Poland.

A combat report by 1./PzRgt 1, dated 3 September 1939 reads:

> After the seizure of Kamiensk during the afternoon of 3 September 1939, 2.Kp was ordered to guard the heights northeast of the town. A platoon led by _Feldwebel_ Hartmann advanced via Wola Nieszkowska to take the bridge at Rozprza. On reaching an area south of the village his tanks came under fire from enemy positions. Two PzKpfw III were hit several times and badly damaged. Both crews, except for one man, were rescued. Despite being severely injured, Hartmann organized another tank to evacuate the wounded. Although the tanks had been abandoned some distance from our front-line positions a mixed platoon, formed from 2.Kp and 4.Kp, were ordered to attack as cover for the recovery operation. When approaching our disabled tanks, a _Halbzug_ [half platoon], of two PzKpfw IV led by _Leutnant_ von Oertzen came under heavy fire from enemy anti-tank teams and a 75mm gun. Our PzKpfw IVs attacked with high-explosive shells to silence the enemy and then smoke, to allow von Oertzen to organize the evacuation of the remaining casualties. Unfortunately, the two PzKpfw III could not be recovered. During action one PzKpfw IV was hit several times and immobilized, another was halted due to a damaged final-drive unit. Despite this both tanks continued firing and finally managed to silence the 75mm gun position. _Leutnant_ Staudte requested reinforcements by radio. As a consequence, _Oberleutnant_ Philipp was ordered to counterattack with three PzKpfw IV. As darkness obscured the battle area, both PzKpfw IV and PzKpfw II were recovered despite heavy fire from enemy machine gun and artillery positions. The two abandoned PzKpfw III were still burning and could not be retrieved. Rozprza was captured on the next day and both hulks were recovered.

Although the above appears to have been a 'textbook' tank assault, the choice of deploying PzKpfw III for the attack without adequate reconnaissance –

leaving the commander unaware of enemy anti-tank and field gun positions – was a serious mistake which led not only to the loss of two tanks but also a number of casualties.

Also the PzKpfw III Ausf A to Ausf D, which were in service at the time, had 14.5mm front armour and were very susceptible to fire from anything more powerful than an armour-piercing (rifle) bullet, whereas the majority of PzKpfw IV were already fitted with 30mm armour. But the commander, although aware of the weakness, was duty bound to deploy whatever he had available to achieve his given objective.

In 1939, the HWa continued to regard the PzKpfw III as a main battle tank and showed no inclination to halt production.

On 1 October 1939, a junior officer from 3.PzDiv submitted an experience report:

The crew of PzKpfw IV Ausf C go about their task of daily maintenance. Due to the prominent white cross being used by Polish anti-tank gunners as an aiming point, most crews either overpainted or obliterated them with mud.

Combat in forests and built up areas:
Once again it has been made obvious that Panzer units should avoid combat in forests and most towns. However, those with houses built from wood were easily set on fire with high-explosive rounds fired from 7.5cm-armed PzKpfw. The subsequent blaze would force any Polish troops out into open, where we shot them down with our machine gun fire. I am convinced that the 7.5cm-armed PzKpfw is the perfect support vehicle for infantry in urban warfare.

Observed from an open cross-country car of an infantry unit, a Polish village is left in flames after an attack by a German tank company. Note the two PzKpfw IV.

The report continues:

> The 7.5cm gun has proven to be an excellent weapon. It is clear that all future development should concentrate on this tank [PzKpfw IV], since it has been a great success in many battles.

After the conclusion of the Polish campaign, 2.leDiv submitted a report of their experiences:

> Organization: The light division was a valuable asset during the Polish campaign. Their firepower proved sufficiently effective to fulfill many missions [advance to the Vistula]. Its main advantage over a standard Panzer division is the ability to be quickly transferred over distances of 500km and more.
> The tank battalion: neither the PzKpfw I nor the PzKpfw II is sufficiently armoured. The Polish anti-tank rifle can penetrate even the front armour of a PzKpfw II Ausf D [30mm] at a range of 100m. We suggest equipping the light division with only the PzKpfw IV, but arming it with a lighter weapon and deploying it as a reconnaissance vehicle for a Panzer division.

Although the commander extolls the efficiency and effectiveness of his light division, military planners had already decided to convert all units into standard Panzer divisions. He also notes the performance of the Polish 7.9mm *Karabin przeciwpancerny UR wzór* (anti-tank rifle 'Uruguay' model) 35: the weapon had a ballistic performance comparable to others firing similar size ammunition, including the German *Panzerbüchse* PzB 38. Finally, it is interesting to note that he advocates the division being equipped with only one type; the PzKpfw IV.

Officials at the HWa decided in late 1939 that there would be no changes to how a Panzer division was to be equipped and clearly stated that there would be no further discussions.

After the Polish army surrendered and the country was occupied, most Panzer divisions returned to their home garrison and settled into their normal routine including manoeuvres and training exercises using experience gained in recent fighting.

Although *Fall Weiss* was a short campaign a number of tanks were lost. The *Rüststand* published in November 1939, notes the loss of 70 PzKpfw IV, but this figure includes those damaged beyond repair in accidents and also those returned to Germany to be refurbished.

A PzKpfw IV Ausf A has received two lethal hits; one has destroyed the MG gun mounting, the other has penetrated the 14.5mm front armour. Such light damage could be quickly repaired, even by the limited facilities at a divisional workshop.

PzKpfw IV production 1939

January	16	119
February	17	135
March	16	152
April	11	168
May	11	179
June	10	190
July	11	200
August	10	211
September	0	211
October	20	192
November	11	212
December	14	223

The crew of a PzKpfw IV Ausf B use a fire hose to wash their vehicle. Although not considered to be essential, most considered washing it necessary since it could prolong the life of the running gear.

1940 – *Fall Gelb*

The invasion of Poland ended on 6 October 1939, and the Panzer divisions began the process of re-equipping to full strength in preparation for *Fall Gelb* (Case Yellow); a second *Blitzkreig,* but this time through The Low Countries and into France. More importantly, all combat experience reports were compiled in terms of containing detail of tactics, weaponry and organization. Once collated, instruction pamphlets were produced and distributed to the commanders of combat training units. Driver training was given the highest priority.

On 10 March 1940 *Oberst* Werner, the commander of PzRgt 31, issued a memorandum:

> 1) The PzKpfw III and PzKpfw IV can be handed over to new drivers only after they have received comprehensive instruction and been thoroughly trained. It is important to make clear that both tanks have fundamentally different driving characteristics.
> 2) During instruction, new drivers must be made aware that both PzKpfw III and PzKpfw IV are much larger and heavier than the PzKpfw II.

One of the problems facing instruction units was that many of the recruits came from rural areas in Germany; the majority could not drive and many had not even had close contact with a motor vehicle. As the war progressed, tank driver training continued to be affected by an ever-present shortage of suitable vehicles and fuel. Another problem the Panzer divisions had to face was that many replacement drivers supplied from training units had received only basic instruction which caused many front-line units to train drivers in the field. Many after-action reports refer to the lack of driving skills, especially in young drivers, as the main reason for many avoidable losses.

The commander of a PzKpfw IV from 10.PzDiv greets the commander of an infantry unit after the occupation of Calais, an important port on the Channel coast, on 26 May 1940. (Getty)

In the winter 1939/40, PzRgt 31 was ordered to escort a motorized column for a distance of some 130km. The route was covered in deep in snow which was cleared but the surface quickly iced over as the temperature dropped to -20 degrees centigrade. In general, their virtually new tanks performed well, but were not equipped for such conditions: in accordance with regulations, the cleats fitted to the tracks proved to be useful in snow, but not on ice-covered roads, especially those with a steep camber. The cleats, which were made from cast iron, quickly wore out and had a tendency to fracture in the severe cold. If the cleats were left on when the tank was being driven over a firm surface, severe vibrations occurred and caused damage to the running gear.

Standard engine oil proved to be unsuitable in severe winter conditions. The electric-powered starter motor could not turn a very cold engine; the crew would have to use the manually operated inertia starter. Unfortunately, though a special oil for winter conditions may have alleviated the problem, none was available at the time.

Fuel consumption rose significantly as the temperature plummeted. During rest periods it was necessary for the crew to start the engine every two hours and let it run for 20 minutes.

February 1940: A PzKpfw IV Ausf C, carrying rudimentary winter camouflage made from white sheets and paint. Note the radio operator's visor has been blanked over with a small sheet of metal plate.

During the march, a PzKpfw IV, nine PzKpfw II, five PzKpfw I and a kl PzBefw (SdKfz 265) were affected by a number of mechanical failures, as were a number of the soft-skinned vehicles. It was also noted that PzRgt 31 consumed some 10,000 to 12,000 litres of fuel each day.

As part of their preparations for the invasion of France, German forces completed a large number of realistic combat exercises. Many tactical lessons were learnt and then compiled in training documents; most were distributed to the commanders of PzKpfw IV.

A report prepared by the regimental staff of PzRgt 31 stated:

A surprisingly large number (approximately 30) PzKpfw IV Ausf A to Ausf D of an unknown Panzer division have been assembled in a German city prior to the western campaign.

Before the tank assault is initiated, all our PzKpfw IV must be deployed in a tactical formation. An open field of vision is essential if we are to provide accurate fire support. Good camouflage is also indispensable.

Fire support from the PzKpfw IV is an absolute prerequisite for any tank assault.

The PzKpfw IV is more effective on the battlefield than an artillery battery. Their firepower, if methodically and selectively used, can break any resistance. Thanks to the tank chassis being a stable platform, fire from the PzKpfw IV is very accurate. The 7.5cm KwK, when firing effective high-explosive ammunition, is capable of eliminating most enemy anti-tank gun positions.

The PzKpfw IV is suitable for attacking those cells of enemy resistance the divisional

artillery cannot and without a great expenditure of ammunition. But, limited ammunitions stowage in the vehicle, requires selective and accurate targeting. Resupply during a battle will not be possible. Rapid fire must only be used in an emergency situation.

The medium tank company has to monitor combat of the light tank company (PzKpfw II and PzKpfw III). During combat, the medium tank company must closely follow the tanks of the light company and be ready to intervene where and when this is necessary.

The remarks regarding the accuracy of the 7.5cm KwK are interesting and contradict some general preconceptions. Unfortunately, the author of the report does not mention any range figures, but it must be assumed that the PzKpfw IV would have been positioned beyond the range of enemy anti-tank defence (600m). The standard procedure for the gunner of a PzKpfw IV was to 'bracket' a target; an experienced man could hit a target with the third round.

Technical Progress

Production of the next batch of PzKpfw IV was initiated in October 1939, but the original dated back to 1938, when 200 were ordered as 4./BW. However, Hitler almost immediately demanded an additional batch (5./BW) of 48

Above: Winter 1939/1940: A PzKpfw IV Ausf A in front of a PzKpfw IV Ausf B; both have large red-painted numerals, outlined in white, applied to the turret and front plate. The vehicle number, 831, is painted on a metal plate mounted on the side of the superstructure.

Far left: Although early models of the PzKpfw IV had a *Fliegerbeschussgerät* (anti-aircraft mounting) fitted on the left-hand side of the superstructure, a member of the crew has fabricated a simpler mounting for the 7.92mm MG 34. The gun is fitted with a *Patronentrommel* (saddle drum) magazine.

Right: The PzKpfw IV Ausf D had a number of improvements; the 7.5cm KwK L/24 gun was fitted with an armoured mantlet and a *Maschinengewehr* (MG – machine gun) 34 was installed in the hull. The turret number '531' indicates the the tank is in service with 5.Kp and this is confirmed by the marking adjacent to the driver's visor.

PzKpfw IV to equip units of the Waffen-SS. In January 1940, the *Allgemeines Heeresamt* (AHA – general army office) overruled the Fuhrer and ordered – because of the 'critical war situation' – all vehicles to be delivered directly to the Heer (army). Subsequently both production batches were then combined and designated PzKpfw IV Ausf D.

It is almost certain that general production problems in Germany industry were also a reason for this decision. The *Rüststand* (armaments situation report) dated November 1939, showed an optimistic production target of some 50 BW each month (this was not achieved until October 1941). A more realistic figure of 20 was given for the period January to May 1940, which increased to 30 units in the preceding months.

In May 1940, the ordnance department investigated the problem and found that Krupp-Grusonwerke was plagued by the same problems that were endemic throughout the German armaments industry.

- Problems caused by the last winter: restricted supplies of coal, oil and gas, and a serious lack of transport.
- A general shortage of workers at Krupp-Grusonwerke and many of its subcontractors; large numbers had been conscripted into the military.
- A shortfall in the supply of raw materials and a lack of replacement or new machinery.

Above: Several PzKpfw IV Ausf B and a PzKpfw III Ausf C on the gunnery training range in early 1940.

Far left: A training exercise prior to the *Blitzkrieg* (lightning war) on France: A PzKpfw IV Ausf A of 2.PzDiv is about to cross a waterway over which pioneers have used *Übergangsschienen* (bridging sections) to construct a simple but effective bridge.

A Pzkpfw IV Ausf C
passes through Châlons-
sur-Marne in May 1940.
The tank is in service
with 8.Kp of PzRgt 11
(6.PzDiv).

PzKpfw IV production 1940

		Total Stock (inc. *Brückenleger*)
January	20	237
February	20	257
March	24	270
April	20	280
May	20	290
June	23	236
July	26	241
August	30	274
September	17	300
October	30	324
November	30	353
December	30	386

Left: An engineer makes adjustments to the bands of the steering brake in a PzKpfw IV Ausf A. Note the simple driver's visor.

The AHA confirmed that it required Krupp-Grusonwerke to increase production of the BW to 30 units each, but this would be dependent on the availability of the workforce. In 1941, it became obvious to officials at the AHA that to achieve the projected output (and any increases), other companies would have to be contracted to produce the PzKpfw IV.

The PzKpfw IV Ausf D incorporated a number of improvements and included better armour protection; the sides and rear of the hull, the superstructure and also the turret were now fabricated from 20mm plate, but the *Bugpanzer* (front plate) remained at 30mm. A ball-mounted MG 34 – removed on the Ausf B and Ausf C – was positioned as before in the front of the superstructure and the gun mantlet was fitted with a protective armour plate.

PzKpfw IV Ausf D, (no add-on armour)
Weight:	20,320kg
Engine:	Maybach HL120 TRM
Performance:	265hp
Speed (maximum):	40kph
Range (road):	210km
Range (cross country):	130km
Trench crossing:	2.3m
Fording depth:	80cm
Ground clearance:	40cm

A pontoon-type ferry assembled from *Brückengerät* 'B' bridging sections. Four types could be built, light (4,064kg capacity), medium (12,192kg) and heavy (24,384kg). Propulsion was simple; troops rowed using long paddles. A group of pioneers observe from a grosse *Flossäck* (large inflatable) 34.

Increased Armour

Long before the PzKpfw IV Ausf D entered production the *Waffenamt*, and other departments of the army, had already received and evaluated the first wartime experience reports. In general, those on the frontline thought the PzKpfw IV to be an excellent tank, but the majority underlined a request for the vehicle to have better armour protection. Many reports emanated from veterans of the Polish campaign.

The *Waffenamt* commented on this problem in a letter dated 25 October 1939:

As for C, PzKpfw

a) Any reinforcement of the armour is only possible for the *Bugpanzer* (front plate) on the hull. It will not be possible on the front of the turret.

b) A permanent reinforcement of the front armour can only be made on production vehicles, but this will require fundamental changes during construction. However, it is certainly possible. The front of the superstructure remains a problem; any increase in weight is unacceptable. The turret would have to be re-engineered to have thicker armour, but again any increase in weight cannot be accepted.

c) Moreover, any such modifications could not be incorporated on production vehicles until 1941. But that is when the new PzKpfw VI is scheduled to enter production and this model has been designed with heavier armour.

d) *Heereswaffenamt* has made the following comment: (A) The front plate armour on production tanks should be increased to 50mm. (B) Bolt extra armour [appliqué] on the front of the superstructure to provide 50mm of protection. (C) The turret front cannot be strengthened.

The PzKpfw IV Ausf A was fitted with a fold-out *Fliegerbeschussgerät* (anti-aircraft mounting) on the left-hand side of the superstructure, but traverse was limited which hindered firing at low-flying aircraft.

The letter indicates that any increase of the armour during production was almost impossible. The BW was originally designed as medium-class (18,000kg) tank and any reinforcement of the armour would result in an increase in weight, whenever it was fitted. [The 'new tank' referred to is the PzKpfw VI Tiger Ausf E heavy tank which was undergoing trials as the Henschel VK 36.01 and would enter service at army group level in 1942. But it would never replace the BW nor the PzKpfw IV.]

A number of trials were conducted at military testing grounds with additional (corresponding) weights fitted – to simulate a gross weight of 21,750kg – and no problems were experienced with the running gear, suspension or transmission. But engineers found that the maximum road speed must be reduced to 25kph.

Above: A PzKpfw IV Ausf C being driven on to a SSys *schwerer Plattformwagen* (heavy flat-bed car). The German military favoured rail transport to avoid the mechanical perils of a long march to a battlefront. The tanks have no markings, possibly to conceal the identity of the unit during the transfer.

Right: A *Deutsche Reichsbahn* (German State Railways) standard four-axle goods wagon had a capacity of 26,420kg, which was sufficient to carry a PzKpfw IV. The tank is in service with 1.PzDiv.

Following a proposal from the HWa, the industry developed and began producing *appliqué* (add-on) 'armour kits' for the PzKpfw IV which could be fitted by workshop units:

- 30mm riveted-on armour for the 30mm hull front
- 30mm bolted-on armour for the front of the superstructure
- 20mm bolted-on armour for the side of the hull
- 20mm bolted-on armour for the side superstructure

The 'armour kit' was designed so that it could be fitted to PzKpfw IV Ausf B and Ausf C, but some alterations had to be made to fit the earlier Ausf A. In June 1940, Krupp-Grusonwerke was ordered, by the HWa, to make preparations for fitting add-on armour on vehicle in production. But for reasons unknown, the department repeatedly postponed their order until July. The result: none of the PzKpfw IV deployed for *Fall Weiss* were fitted with add-on armour.

Records prepared at the *Waffenamt* show the numbers of PzKpfw IV fitted add-on armour as follows:

Two PzKpfw IV, from 6.PzDiv, loaded on an SSys *schwerer Plattformwagen* (heavy flatbed car), which had a capacity of 50,800kg, ready to be returned to Germany for repair and a general overhaul. The *Seitenvorgelage* (final drive) unit, which often failed, has been removed from both tanks.

A PzKpfw IV Ausf D of 7.PzDiv, crosses a *Brückengerät* 'B' built over the river Meuse (Maas) at speed. This versatile bridging system had a maximum capacity of 24,384kg. Each bridging unit had 31 trailers, for carrying pontoons, and a number of trucks and heavy half-track tractors

Ausf A:	35
Ausf B:	42
Ausf C:	140
Ausf D:	248
Ausf E:	223

Although the above corresponds with the total number of BW tanks ordered, any discrepancies have possibly occurred due to any vehicle lost during the Polish and French campaigns, having not been recorded.

PzKpfw IV Ausf D (with add-on armour)

Weight:	21,740kg
Engine:	Maybach HL120 TRM
Performance:	265hp
Speed (maximum):	40kph
Range (road):	210km
Range (cross country):	130km
Trench crossing:	2.3m
Fording depth:	80cm
Ground clearance:	40cm

Many of the add-on armour kits were fabricated, and often fitted, by specialist armour manufacturers, and the manufacturers began to fit the *appliqué* armour on any PzKpfw IV Ausf D currently on the assembly line. The add-on armour was fitted on all PzKpfw IV Ausf E from the very beginning of production.

But the planned introductions would be delayed due to a shortage of armour plate. [Photographs taken during the war, including Barbarossa, show that many PzKpfw IV Ausf D had only the brackets fitted.]

Changes in Organization

On 1 September 1939, a new organizational structure KStN 1175 *Sonderstärke* (Sd – special strength) was published. It detailed a unit equipped only with the PzKpfw IV (plus a few PzKpfw II), and was now called *mittlere Panzerkompanie* (m PzKp – medium tank company) replacing the previous le PzKp 'a'. The m PzKp was to have an authorized strength of 14 PzKpfw IV in three platoons and five PzKpfw II as a light platoon. The PzKpfw III was similarly issued to the new le PzKp in accordance with KStN 1171 (Sd), which showed 17 PzKpfw III and five PzKpfw II.

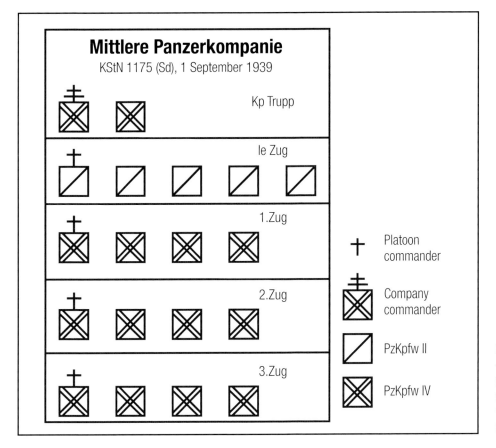

In 1940, the new structure – KStN 1175 (Sd) – authorized a medium tank company to have 14 PzKpfw IV and five PzKpfw II.

A recovery team of PzRgt 8 (10.PzDiv) crosses a purpose-built bridge over a French river. The SdKfz 9 is attached to a SdAnh 116 carrying a PzKpfw IV: note the 'Wolfsangel' symbol on the mudguard (fender).

All active Panzer divisions received orders to implement this structure. But an insufficient number of PzKpfw IV (and PzKpfw III) would allow only a gradual conversion. By May 1940, it was intended for all Panzer divisions to have one medium tank company for each battalion and supported by two light tank companies in accordance with KStN 1175 (Sd).

In reality, no Panzer division could be issued with the authorized number of 14 PzKpfw IV for each m PzKp (Sd) and numerous panzer divisions could never be equipped as intended.

Another problem was that many of the *Heereszeugämter* (HZA – army vehicle depots) were struggling to replace combat losses and were unable to supply the tanks necessary to comply with the new structure.

In March 1940, Major Thomale of the *Oberkommando des Heeres* (OKH – Army High Command) informed the commander of PzRgt 31, *Oberst* Werner, of a fundamental change to the organization and strength of the tank companies in his regiment in compliance with the new *Sonderstärke*-type KStN.

Those companies equipped with PzKpfw III and PzKpfw IV tanks would now be replaced by more specialized companies equipped with either the

Two PzKpfw IV of 6.PzDiv at the beginning of the autumn *Rasputitsa* (mud season) in Russia. A lack of surfaced roads forced German tank crews to use tracks which were only suitable for horse transport.

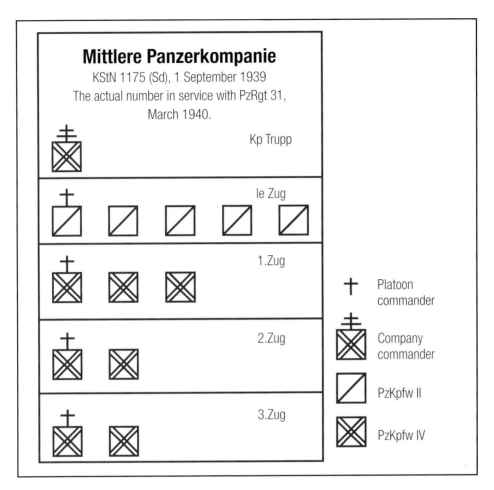

Mittlere Panzerkompanie
KStN 1175 (Sd), 1 September 1939
The actual number in service with PzRgt 31,
March 1940.

Kp Trupp

le Zug

1.Zug

2.Zug

3.Zug

†   Platoon commander

Company commander

PzKpfw II

PzKpfw IV

During the French campaign there were never enough tanks to completely implement the KStN 1175 (Sd).

PzKpfw III or the PzKpfw IV. The reasoning behind this reorganization is not known, but there were many benefits to be had by reducing the number of tank types within the company from four (le PzKp 'a', KStN 1175 dated 1 October 1938) to only two.

Major Thomale evaluated the number of available PzKpfw IV in the regiment and suggested the new structure could be adapted in view of the number of tanks held. Subsequently, he decided that each of the two medium PzKp were to be equipped with five PzKpfw II and eight PzKpfw IV.

These fundamental changes were applied in different ways from one tank division to another and the problem was further exacerbated by the slow pace at which new tanks were being produced.

It is obvious that the units affected by the 'official' KStN structures treated them simply as a rough guide, since any implementation by a Panzer division was dependent on availability. Obviously, a commander had the freedom to

Two recovery teams from 1.PzDiv; the lead vehicle tows a *Sonderanhänger* (SdAnh – special purpose trailer) 116 carrying a PzKpfw IV Auisf A, the second a PzKpfw II. The oak leaf emblem used by the division is visible on the mudguard (fender) as is the letter 'W' for *Werkstatt* (workshop).

Tank strength as of 10 May 1940, *Fall Gelb*

Type	Number
PzKpfw I	554
PzKpfw II	920
PzKPfw 35(t)	118
PzKpfw 38(t)	207
PzKpfw III	349
PzKpfw IV	280
PzBefWg	154
StuG	30

move his tanks from unit to unit as vehicles suffered from mechanical problems or were lost in combat.

In the case of PzRgt 31, the restructuring of their light PzKp and medium PzKp was performed in some haste during the first two weeks of April, since the regiment was to be part of the force deployed for *Fall Gelb*. A similar effort was given to adapting the maintenance and mechanical services to comply with the new structure.

After-action Reports:

The commander of 3./PzRgt 31, *Hauptmann* Freiherr von Vietunghoff, submitted this report after a fierce fight at Le Quesnoy during the advance on Douai and then Cambrai:

> 8 May 1940: Maubeuge had been taken in the early morning hours after a daring surprise raid by II.Abt. Later the enemy launched a desperate counterattack, but this was repelled by 3.Kp of the *Rote Teufel* [Red Devils]. This was followed by a short, but fierce, tank-versus-tank duel between two tanks both firing armour-piercing rounds at each other at a range of 80m. The PzKpfw IV was a hundredth of a second

The crew of this PzKpfw IV Ausf B has disobeyed strict orders and positioned sections of track on their tank for extra protection. French anti-tank gunners were particularly effective when fighting in cities.

For an unknown reason, a long section of track has been stowed on the engine cover of this PzKpfw IV Ausf B. The distinctive Bison symbol, stencilled on the side of the turret, indicates that it is in service with PzRgt 7 (10.PzDiv).

quicker, and the commander proudly reported by radio: "Last enemy resistance broken, tank enemy shot down". However, there was hardly any time for our tanks pause: it is like being on an express train, one minute we are almost stopped, and then we are rushing forward again.

We advanced across the fields towards Valenciennes and the spearhead was formed by 3.Kp [one of the two heavy companies]. I noticed that our supply column, travelling by road, had halted. Before I could ask why, I heard firing; our reconnaissance battalion was in combat with enemy forces positioned to defend Villereux.

Since my superior officer was attending a meeting at high command. I had to make the decision. I ordered my company to bypass our columns to go to the aid of the reconnaissance battalion. Despite the difficult terrain we reached them a short distance from Villereux.

After contacting the commander, I suggested a plan for an attack, with which he agreed. Just two minutes later, the platoon commanders received their respective orders, then 1.Zug [PzKpfw IV] rushed towards the enemy. The French anti-tank guns were a serious problem: we knew that he who held his nerve and fired more accurately would win with the first round. Then I heard the first three rounds being fired from our PzKpfw IV and a radio message followed: "Enemy anti-tank gun

positions destroyed, and his troops are retreating through Villereux. 1.Zug is to advance". In this situation I ordered the entire company to follow. On reaching our advance party we managed to push the enemy back far beyond the village. I had only a few moments to decide on how to continue the attack.

Suddenly, I noticed a further enemy force of tanks, anti-tank guns and infantry advancing from the left flank to attack our position; approximated. A thousand ideas rushed through my mind; the enemy must not succeed in regaining his lost territory. Now they shall get to know our Red Devils; I am filled with rage seeing this bunch of African soldiers lying opposite our lines each wearing a red fez. Today we will settle old scores; the French 'gentlemen' shall experience our concentrated hatred. A short radio message leads the tank company into the new direction.

The radio operators did not need their *Funktafeln* (radio documents) anymore, since they had learned the platoon's code names by heart. 1.Zug advanced to the forest on the right, 2.Zug marched to the left, my *Führerpanzer* [command tank] as the *Kompanietrupp* [company headquarters] in the centre – jump up, go, go – up and get them. I have a good view from my *Führerkuppel* [commander´s cupola] as our tanks opened-out into a broad formation and accelerate towards the enemy.

Shells are bursting everywhere; anti-tank rounds rip up the ground. We know our target and rush ahead. The Fischer platoon are positioned to my right; they have

Each Panzer division engaged during the French campaign had a small number of PzKpfw II Ausf C which, despite having thin armour, were often used by a battalion or regimental commander.

been ordered to defend the flank. I listen to the satisfying 'cough' as our 7.5cm gun fires. The shooting becomes wilder and wilder.

The temperature in my tank reached 50 degrees centigrade. The air is contaminated by cordite gases and toxic smelling fumes from the steering brakes, transmission and gearbox; the inside of our tank has turned into hell. The hands of the driver cling to the rubber grips of the steering levers. The wireless operator, his face dirty and bathed in sweat, sends message after message in a clear and loud voice.

I can see four enemy tanks approaching, but they are out of range. We try to stalk them like a fox by making best use of the cover provided by the hedgerow. On reaching the edge, we become more alert, aware that enemy anti-tank gunners might be waiting for us. I decide to pass the edge at full speed, hoping to shock the enemy. Quite often they abandon their weapon and flee for their lives.

Now we are close enough to engage the enemy tanks. Range 800, *Kopfgranate rot*, fire! We fire round after round from our barrel just as if we are on the on the training grounds. The first tank catches fire, which causes the crew of a second to abandon the vehicle and flee. Suddenly I notice a fierce explosion behind us. A tank of the Fischer platoon has been hit in the fuel tank. I hope that the crew was able to get out unharmed, but I must concentrate on the battle. After another 30 minutes

A PzKpfw IV Ausf D carries the symbol, two white crosses, of 9.PzDiv. A fascine – a bundle of brushwood – is attached to the rear of the turret; a detail often seen on the tanks of 9.PzDiv.

of fighting the enemy assault has been successfully repelled. There are casualties everywhere, and many French soldiers surrender and approach with their arms raised. The success was great; half an artillery battery and four tanks have been destroyed and several anti-tank guns knocked out. Large numbers of enemy supply trucks have been destroyed and are blocking the roads.

The comment made by von Vietinghoff in regard to the African soldiers reflects an attitude that was endemic amongst many in wartime Germany: '*deutsche Herrenrasse*' (German master race).

It is noteworthy that the PzKpfw IV-equipped medium tank company formed the spearhead of this assault although this tactic was strictly against orders. Possibly, von Vietinghoff decided that the 7.5cm gun mounted in the PzKpfw IV would be more effective against enemy anti-tank guns than the 3.7cm in the PzKpfw III. A note in the report shows that many of the tank-versus-tank duels were fought at close range, some 80m to 150m.

The report also clearly indicates that German middle-ranking officers were encouraged to be highly flexible in their decision making on the battlefield.

After fighting their way through The Low Countries, 9.PzDiv with PzRgt 33 became part of the force deployed to contain what remained of the British Expeditionary Force (BEF) waiting to be evacuated from Dunkirk. The unit was then ordered to Amiens from where it fought in a number of battles before reaching Lyon in July 1940.

The rapid advance across northern Europe had proved that the tactics developed and practiced before the war were correct and were enhanced by experience gained in Poland. Many battles were decided by the momentum of attack, with French commanders squandering large parts of their resources to guard flanks while ignoring those sectors under threat. But the war diary of PzRgt 33 notes that French and British infantry were brave and fought with a stubborn determination, particularly when in well-prepared defensive positions.

French anti-tank mines were a constant threat, but were often deployed carelessly. Their engineers laid mines, always six in a row, which were easy to see and straightforward to clear. But, if a tank did drive over one, then all six would detonate: the regiment lost five tanks to French mines.

The PzKpfw IV crews were often called on to provide support fire for the rifle regiment:

> Any enemy infantry fighting from positions in houses were attacked with 7.5cm gun and machine gun fire. Beside having a massive explosive impact, which blew-out windows and doors, the detonation of the 7.5cm round also had a great effect on morale.

Engineers at a *Feldworkstatt* (field workshop), inspect the crankshaft of a Maybach HL 120 TRM engine which has been removed from the PzKpfw IV in the background.

Above: The complete tracks of this PzKpfw IV Ausf D from 7.PzDiv have been removed in order to check the track pins.

Right: A well-camouflaged PzKpfw IV from 2.PzDiv: note the white symbol with two small white dots.

Above: The *Seitenvorgelage* (final drive), an assembly of planetary, epicyclic and spur gears, was the weak point of the PzKpfw IV tank.

Left: The PzKpfw IV had a fuel capacity of 470 litres. Crews often commandeered supplies from civilian sources during the advance across France.

PzRgt 33 used elaborate tactics when fighting through built-up areas. When moving through the wider streets of a city, up to seven tanks were assembled as small combat groups:

> A single tank advancing as lead vehicle in an urban environment [Amiens] was often quickly halted by the enemy firing from all sides. The guns could not be quickly detected and therefore were not engaged. For this reason, we deployed a row of three tanks [PzKpfw IV] moving side by side through the streets. The lead tank would monitor and fight any target on the road ahead; to guard the flanks, the tank on the left would turn the turret to 9 o'clock, the tank to the right would have the turret at the 3 o'clock position. When crossing a junction, the flanking tanks would be immediately able to open fire on any enemy forces lying in ambush. In one such action, ten enemy anti-tank guns and artillery piece were defeated for the loss of only one tank. All infantry armed with machine guns and positioned in buildings were engaged with 7.5cm KwK and machine-gun fire; some houses were set on fire. The effect on their morale was devastating.

The PzKpfw IV Ausf D was fitted with an armoured gun mantlet and an antenna deflector. The hull machine gun, fired by the radio operator, was an important asset for fighting enemy infantry.

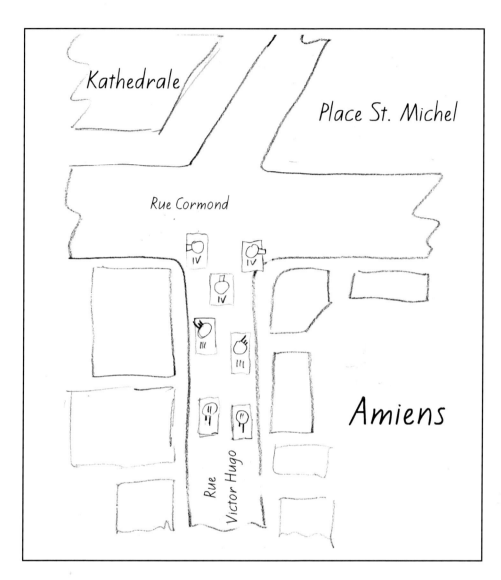

Two further tanks [PzKpfw III] would follow, ready to fire their machine guns at enemy troops firing from a higher floor or a roof. The rear of the formation was protected by two tanks [PzKpfw II] with their turrets turned to the 6 o'clock position ready to suppress a surprise attack.

At the end of the French campaign, a questionnaire was delivered to all Panzer divisions involved in the operation. The commander of PzRgt 33 contributed the following experiences of tank-versus-tank combat:

> PzRgt 33 was involved in only a few in tank-versus-tank actions. Near St.Germain, II./ PzRgt 33 encountered 12 enemy tanks of the type Char B1 bis and a Char 2C [FMC-

A PzKpfw IV Ausf C passes through a French town. The 7.5cm KwK L/24 gun was a useful weapon for urban warfare when firing high-explosive ammunition against enemies positioned in buildings.

2C]. The battalion had light tanks, but also a PzKpfw III and a PzKpfw IV, and only these were used to attack the enemy tanks. Shots fired at 800m range against the Char 2C had no effect. But two of the other tanks were effectively attacked at 400m to 500m range. Our high-explosive shells damaged their tracks and the turrets were easily blocked by hits. After the fight, we inspected the vehicles and found that our high-explosive shells, fired without a delay fuse, were ineffective. Even the 7.5cm KopfGr rot armour-piercing shells did not penetrate the armour at 500m. Enemy tanks of the type R 35 were easily penetrated at 150m range by the 3.7cm KwK.

The report continues:

The enemy anti-tank defences, if they had enough time to get into position, were appropriately deployed and often effectively camouflaged. Often they would be positioned at the edge of woodland and at junctions or roadblocks. The enemy 4.7cm anti-tank gun is fitted with effective armour which is impervious to 7.92mm armour-piercing rifle ammunition. The French anti-tank gunners often did not fire at the first wave of our tanks, but opened fire, at close range, on the following tanks often inflicting heavy casualties.

The 7.5cm KwK L/24 gun mounted in the PzKpfw IV was a most valuable asset and completely fulfilled all expectations during the invasion of France.

Attached to the report was a note on the reliability of the tanks used by PzRgt 33:

> All available PzKpfw I failed due to various mechanical breakdowns; a number could not be repaired. The PzKpfw II proved to be mechanically much better. The PzKpfw III suffered many significant breakdowns, most involving the Variorex gearbox. The front running wheels show heavy wear due to the tank being front heavy. Finally, the PzKpfw IV performed well in general.

Although the PzKpfw I was considered to be obsolete, the vehicle was used in relatively large numbers; PzRgt 33 alone had a compliment of 56 at the beginning of the invasion. The design differences between the Daimler-Benz-built PzKpfw

A column of PzKpfw IV Ausf C has halted in a tree-lined avenue of a French town. The horse-drawn wagons appear to have been recently abandoned as French forces made a hasty retreat.

Marshy terrain was a danger to armoured formations. For this reason, German tanks carried a fascine – a bundle of brushwood – ready to roll out. Here a PzKpfw IV rolls off some *Übergangsschienen* (bridging sections) down onto a *Cordstrasse* (corduroy road) – known as such since it resembled the ribbed cloth.

A PzKpfw IV of 6.PzDiv being ferried across the Meuse (Maas) during the early stages of *Fall Gelb*. The border region between Germany and France was crisscrossed with streams, rivers and wide canals which tested pioneer units to the limit.

III and Krupp-built PzKpfw IV were more significant than expected. In some respects, the PzKpfw III was mechanically more sophisticated; the torsion bar suspension, with internally mounted hydraulic shock absorbers, gave the type excellent cross-country performance, but it was very susceptible to damage. The tank was fitted with a Maybach Variorex ten-speed semi-automatic gearbox which, although a mechanical masterpiece, often failed and was not simple to repair. (The PzKpfw III Ausf H was to be fitted with a conventional ZF SSG 77 six-speed gearbox.) The Maybach HL 120 TRM engine was fitted with a governor to restrict performance, but the tank could still be driven at close to 65kph, often becoming dangerously unstable.

The suspension designed for the PzKpfw IV was a more conventional eight-wheel type fitted with external leaf springs. Although less comfortable for the crew when traversing rough terrain, it did provide a more stable gun platform and was also more reliable. From the beginning of production, Krupp-Grusonwerke fitted the type with a ZF SSG 76 six-speed manually operated gearbox. Consequently, the PzKpfw IV suffered significantly fewer mechanical problems.

A column of tanks from 5.PzDiv led by a Pzkpfw IV Ausf C. Note the access hatches for the steering brakes have been opened due to the summer heat.

French anti-tank defences posed a constant and often dangerous threat to all German tank crews.

From a report sent in by PzRgt 33:

> None of our tanks were safe from enemy anti-tank gunfire at ranges below 600m. The PzKpfw I and PzKpfw II were easily defeated by the 2.5cm Hotchkiss at various ranges. The British Boys anti-tank rifle was effective for defeating PzKpfw I and PzKpfw II, but only at close range. But the PzKpfw III and PzKpfw IV were impervious to fire from the 2.5cm Hotchkiss anti-tank gun.

The majority of the PzKpfw III and PzKpfw IV deployed for the French campaign had 30mm frontal armour. The standard French anti-tank weapon, the Hotchkiss-built 25mm [2.5cm] *Canon Léger de 25 Antichar SA-L modele* 1937, could penetrate 30mm of armour, but only under favourable conditions. When fired at the side of a PzKpfw III and PzKpfw IV it could be lethal at up to 1,000m range.

The 47mm [4.7cm] Canon de 47 *Antichar modele* 1937 was a much more powerful anti-tank gun which could defeat all German tanks at up to 1,000m range, including those with 30mm front armour. Fortunately for German tank crews very few had been delivered to the French army.

From a questionnaire delivered to 10.PzDiv:

Question: How did our tanks prove in combat?
Answer: The PzKpfw IV is mechanically reliable; its weaponry is good and very effective. Armour protection is too weak and offers little or no protection against French 2.5cm and 4.7cm anti-tank guns.
Question: Which enemy weapons were especially effective and were they superior to our weapons?
Answer: The 2.5cm and 4.7cm were most effective; both penetrated the armour on all types of German tanks.

An addition to the questionnaire, notes were added concerning action by the tanks of 10.PzDiv against bunkers:

Commitment of tanks:
10.PzDiv never used tanks systematically against fortifications. Only on one occasion did a PzKp fight bunker positions. But during this commitment the 7.5cm KwK-armed PzKpfw IV proved to be most effective.

The 30mm front armour of a PzKpfw IV could be easily penetrated by French 25mm anti-tank ammunition. Two well-aimed hits have penetrated the armour in front of the driver ripping the visor was from its interior frame: it is unlikely that the driver survived.

PzRgt 2 (1.PzDiv) returned to their home garrison, in the town of Eisenach, Thuringia, after the fall of France. Here a PzKpfw IV Ausf C leads a Pzkpfw II Ausf C through the town square.

In July 1939, the HWa issued an order to Krupp-Grusonwerke for the production of a further batch (6./BW) which were to have modifications required after the invasion of Poland. The most noticeable improvement was that this batch would be produced with 50mm front armour. Production began in late summer 1940, and although the hull had been strengthened, the superstructure remained basically unchanged. But the 30mm *appliqué* armour for the front of the superstructure would be fitted at a later date due to an inadequate supply. Only 200 sets of *appliqué* armour were produced between October 1940 and April 1941.

Variants

A number of nations had bridge-layer vehicles in service before World War II and Germany was no exception. Their *Brückenleger* (armoured bridge layer) was originally very simple and built on the chassis of PzKpfw II, PzKpfw 35(t) and even the obsolete PzKpfw I. In 1939, despite severe financial and industrial difficulties, the HWa ordered the development of more effective bridge layers.

Long before the outbreak of war, military planners at WaPrüf 5 had decided to introduce armoured support vehicles for the *Panzer-Pionierkompanie* (PzPiKp – armoured engineer company) in a Panzer division as part of a *Pionier-und Eisenbahnpionier-Abteilung* (engineer and railway engineers battalion).

The PzPiKp was formed as two *Zerstörungszüge* (destruction platoons), a *Brückenleger-Zug* (bridge-layer platoon), a *schwerer Pionier-Zug* (s PiZg – heavy armoured engineer platoon) and one *leichter Pionier-Zug* (le PiZg – light engineer platoon). Each *Zerstörungszug* was to be issued with five *Ladungsleger* I (demolition charge carrier). The s PiZg was equipped with six SdKfz 251/7 half-track vehicles, and the le PiZg was supplied with six trucks.

The commander of PzRgt, (1.PzDiv), *Oberstleutnant* Koppenburg, temporarily used a PzKpfw IV Ausf A as his command vehicle although it is unlikely to have been fitted with long-range radio equipment.

Each *Brückenleger* platoon was to be equipped with four armoured bridge layers. The PzKpfw IV chassis, possibly because of its size, was selected for conversion. The initial order was for 20 vehicles, which were to be delivered as quickly as possible, with an option for a further 60.

In 1939, Krupp-Grusonwerke had developed a vehicle by utilizing the prototype of their eight-wheeled chassis. After a short series of trials, the type

The proposed formation of a PzPiKp for deployment in *Fall Gelb*.

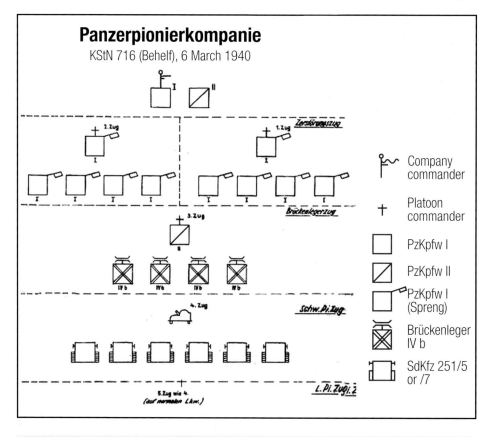

Panzerpionierkompanie

KStN 716 (Behelf), 6 March 1940

Company commander

+ Platoon commander

☐ PzKpfw I

◪ PzKpfw II

PzKpfw I (Spreng)

Brückenleger IV b

SdKfz 251/5 or /7

PzKpfw IV Ausf E

Weight:	22,320kg
Engine:	Maybach HL120 TRM
Performance:	265hp
Speed (maximum):	40kph
Range (road):	210km
Range (cross country):	130km
Trench crossing:	2.3m
Fording depth:	80cm
Ground clearance:	40cm

was ordered into (limited) production. The first order for 20 *Brückenleger* IV 'b' was ready by May 1940 and all were issued to those PzPiKp in 1.PzDiv; 2.PzDiv; 3.PzDiv, 5.PzDiv and 10.PzDiv.

These vehicles were based on PzKpfw IV Ausf C and Ausf D and carried a one-piece 8m long bridging section mounted on two rails which were fitted on top of the tank chassis. By using a system of steel cables and winches, the section, which had a loading capacity of 30,480kg, could be laid and recovered when necessary. Multiple sections would be laid over foldable trestles, to create a longer bridge.

All available *Brückenleger* IV 'b' were deployed for the French campaign, but a number of experience reports indicate that they were not effective due to a number of faults; mainly with the laying mechanism. After the invasion those that survived were withdrawn from service and the chassis repurposed.

The first prototype of the *Brückenleger* IV utilized the chassis – six roadwheels and torsion-bar suspension – designed by Krupp-Grusonwerke for their version of the *Begleitwagen* (BW – escort vehicle) II. The four *Brückenleger* IV 'c' subsequently produced, carried the same bridge-section lifting mechanism: all were issued to 3.PzDiv.

But WaPrüf 5 had already ordered Krupp-Grusonwerke to develop an improved bridge layer. Despite the failings of the first series the company once again chose the PzKpfw IV Ausf D chassis and had completed four *Brückenleger* IV 'c' by January 1941. The bridging section was modified and the vehicle was fitted with an improved winching system. The vehicles were issued to 3.PzDiv ready for deployment in *Unternehmen* Barbarossa.

The development of a specialized bridging vehicle was also initiated in 1939 for use by infantry units. The chassis chosen was the PzKpfw IV Ausf C, fitted with an extendable (up to 30m) ladder, similar to that used by a fire brigade, mounted on the top of the hull. In service the type was known a *Sturmsteg* (assault bridge), but due to production problems the first vehicle was not delivered until end of 1940.

Four assault bridge layers, designated *Brückenleger* IV 's' *Sturmstegpanzer*, were built using the PzKpfw IV Ausf D chassis and supplied to 3.PzDiv for *Unternehmen* Barbarossa.

Two *Infanterie Sturmsteg* (infantry assault bridge) were built, utilizing the PzKpfw IV Auf C chassis, as part of the preparations for *Fall Gelb*. The type was fitted with a fire brigade-type extendable ladder which could bridge a gap some 40m wide to allow infantry to continue their advance.

Above: Two of the 20 *Brückenleger* IV 'b' produced prior to the invasion of France. All were built on refurbished, but old, PzKpfw IV chassis which were mechanically weak and often failed. The later *Brückenleger* IV 'c' proved effective and reliable.

Left: Parts of the bridge-section lifting mechanism on a *Brückenleger* IV 'c'. The *Übergausschinen* (bridging sections) were frequently transported on a *Sonderanhänger* (SdAnh – special purpose trailer) 116 to save the tank chassis.

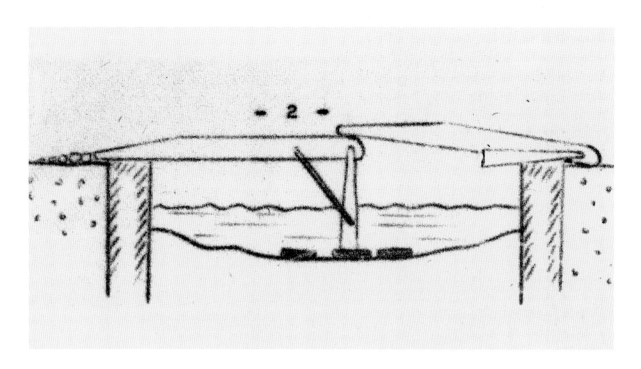

A diagram from a training pamphlet produced by PzPiBtl 39 illustrates how two bridging sections could be used to cross a wider obstacle.

Only a few after-action reports have survived, including this from 3.PzDiv, dated 14 Aug 1941:

> PzPiBtl 39:
> Both types of bridge laying vehicles have proved effective in general. We are convinced that after modification of some the basic shortcomings, every Panzer division should be issued with this bridging equipment.

The basic shortcomings referred to by PzPiBtl 39 included a speed of 18kph which they thought was far was too slow to follow a tank assault. They also complained that the given range of only 40km was completely inadequate and also that many breakdowns were the result of using refurbished chassis. Finally, they noted that many of the problems they experienced with gearboxes, final-drive units and the small-diameter running wheels was due to the chassis being overloaded.

The *Brückenleger* IV 'c' was a great success in combat. On 25 June 1940 an 18m trestle-type bridge was erected over the Sczacara river. This allowed all of the tracked and wheeled vehicles, including elements of a supporting infantry division, to cross as 3.PzDiv and continue the advance.

After this trial deployment for Barbarossa, the *Brückenleger* project was cancelled, since the new tanks being designed or in development would be much, much heavier, weighing some 45,700kg to 61,000kg.

Tauchpanzer (T – Diving Tank)

German offensive strategy heavily relied on the deployment of a strong tank force, which had the weaponry, mobility and armour to rapidly penetrate any defensive positions then attack rear echelons. Most obstacles encountered could be overcome, but deep water would halt any rapid advance. Small rivers and deep streams could be crossed by sections carried on bridge-layer vehicles.

Military planners decided that the only logical solution to the problem was to design or adapt a current type so that it could travel under water.

When Adolf Hitler issued the order to begin preparations for *Unternehmen Seelöwe* (Operation Sea Lion) – his planned invasion of Great Britain – development of an amphibious or submersible tank was expedited. This project was known as *Unterwasser-Kampffahrzeug* (UK – underwater combat vehicle), but a purpose-built vehicle was out of the question due to the ever-present lack of capacity in the armaments industry. Work then began on how to modify or adapt the types currently in service.

The PzKpfw II light tanks could be fitted with flotation pontoons, but the PzKpfw III and PzKpfw IV would have been fitted with auxiliary equipment to

A total of 48 PzKpfw IV Ausf D and an unknown number of PzKpfw IV Ausf E were converted to *Tauchpanzer* (diving tank).

be used as a diving tank. The equipment could not be fitted during production, which resulted in Alkett being contracted to carry out the conversion work.

In August 1940, a total of 52 PzKpfw II with pontoons, 168 PzKpfw III *Tauchpanzer* (T) and 42 PzKpfw IV (T) were ready. Both types of *Tauchpanzer* being prepared for the invasion were fitted with a 15m-long rubber hose supported by an unsinkable float.

On 17 September 1940, Hitler issued the order, '*Unternehmen Seelöwe wird verscohoben*' (Operation Sea Lion is postponed). Subsequently, the diving equipment was removed and placed in storage. In the of spring 1941, a contract was issued to modify a further 105 tanks (PzKpfw III and PzKpfw IV).

This second batch was to be fitted with 3.5m-long steel air pipes to replace the earlier rubber hoses: the same pipes were also provided for the 200 vehicles already converted.

To allow the tanks to travel under water it would be necessary to carry out a number of specified operations: Any bolts or screws which went through the plating were loosened, coated with a sealant and/or hemp and then refastened. Any hinges were sealed with Cosal-Zement – a putty-like compound – and all hatches closed on to a rubber gasket glued around the aperture. To operate under water, this gasket would be coated with a sealant before the hatch was closed and locked. Any narrow gaps around the turret and hull were sealed with rubber solution. The driver's visor was sealed in this way, but also had a large rubber pad glued over the aperture.

The final-drive housings, suspension bearings and those on the return rollers were sealed with sealant-soaked canvas.

A protective flange was welded to the lower edge of the turret which was sealed by an inflatable rubber gasket. A frame fabricated from angle iron was welded on the gun mantlet so that it and the gun could be fitted with a waterproof rubber hood.

The *Panzerführer-Kuppel* (commander's cupola) was also sealed with a rubber hood, but a vision block was left clear as the only means of observation. The entire crew had to use this hatch to enter the vehicle.

The large access hatches for the transmission, steering brakes and engine were sealed with thick rubber seals, and held closed by a toggle lock.

The vents for the engine compartment were framed plating held securely in place by a number of fly nuts.

Finally a hand-operated bilge pump was fitted to remove any water which had entered the fighting and engine compartments.

After completing a diving mission, the turret sealing gasket would be deflated and all hatches in the hull would be forced open. The cover over the gun would be destroyed when the first round was fired.

A *Tauchpanzer* (diving tank) could be used only once and it took several days of laborious work to restore the deep wading capability and it would take a month to prepare for a 15m deep mission.

The available swimming and diving tanks were allotted to number of tank divisions, 3.PzDiv (PzRgt 6); 4.PzDiv (PzRgt 35; 17.PzDiv (PzRgt 39) and 18.PzDiv (PzRgt 18). In June 1941, PzRgt 18 had 36 PzKpfw IV (T) and 3.PzDiv had 12 of the same type. Both 4.PzDiv and 17.PzDiv had the type, but the exact numbers are not known.

In November 1941, consideration was given to fitting the items required for deep wading on PzKpfw IV as they were being assembled. However, the the war situation caused the project be cancelled. Both the PzKpfw V Panther and PzKpfw VI Tiger Ausf E were built with a deep wading capability.

The crew of this *Tauchpanzer* IV Ausf D has not removed the large rubber seal which covered the mantlet and also that over the ball-mounted *Maschinengehwehr* (MG – machine gun) 34.

The *Panzertruppe* would face many important challenges in 1941 and senior officers realized that tactics would have to be improved and, if necessary, changed although the Panzer divisions had already proven to be an effective and vital element in the German war machine. The process was begun by collating all combat experiences and after-action reports from the invasion of Poland – although the defenders had a limited amount of modern weaponry.

One major problem experienced in Poland was the lack of tank-to-tank communication which often affected how units were deployed and fought on the battlefield.

The radio equipment fitted in German tanks was basic and unreliable, a problem exacerbated by operators not receiving adequate instruction and training in radio telephony. This resulted in many orders and tactical instructions being misunderstood, received incomplete or too late to instigate. As a result, the OKW ordered that all units, including the Panzer divisions, were to be thoroughly trained in the use of radio communications: transmitting and receiving messages by voice or Morse and also the use codes. The intensive training began in the winter of 1939 and continued until May 1940: German forces would now be more efficient and thus more effective for the coming *Blitzkrieg* across northern Europe.

During the invasion of Poland, those PzKpfw IV deployed had proven to be mechanically reliable (especially the gearbox and running gear) when compared to the PzKpfw III Ausf E.

An order for the production of a further batch (6./BW) was issued in October 1939. The PzKpfw IV Ausf E incorporated a number of changes which were considered necessary after Poland. The most important was that the hull on all production PzKpfw IV would now be built with 50mm

A PzKpfw IV Ausf E in service with PzRgt 3 (2.PzDiv). Tanks from this regiment can be identified by the two spare running wheels attached to the rear of the turret.

front armour. Interestingly, the last 68 production PzKpfw IV Ausf D had the same armour.

A total of 206 PzKpfw IV Ausf E were built between October 1940 and April 1941, of which four were converted to be used as the chassis for *Brückenleger* IV 'c' and two for use as trials vehicles for *Schachtellaufwerke* (interleaved or overlapping) running gear.

Balkan Campaign

Benito Mussolini, completely ignoring an explicit request from Adolf Hitler, ordered his forces occupying Albania to invade Greece on 28 October 1940. This ill-conceived venture would end in failure since his troops, despite having superior numbers, were halted and forced to retreat: the fighting ceased on 30 April 1940.

In Germany, Hitler had already taken the decision to invade the Soviet Union in the summer of 1941, but he was also acutely aware of the need to keep his southern borders secure. Envoys were sent to the Balkan states to persuade their leaders that it would be advantageous for their countries to join the

PzKpfw IV Ausf E

Weight:	22,350kg
Engine Maybach:	HL120 TRM
Performance:	265hp
Speed (maximum):	40kph
Range (road):	210km
Range (cross country):	130km
Trench crossing:	2.3m
Fording depth:	80cm
Ground clearance:	40cm

Dreimächtepakt (Axis Pact – Germany, Italy and Japan). Hungary and Romania joined in November 1940; followed by Bulgaria and Yugoslavia in March 1941.

But on 27 March 1941, the pro-Axis Tvetkovitch government in Yugoslavia was overthrown in a coup. Almost immediately, the British government declared that it would give full support if Germany invaded. Now Hitler was forced to act and ordered an invasion of Yugoslavia and Greece.

On 6 April 1940, the German armoured formations, 5.PzDiv, 8.PzDiv and 11.PzDiv, positioned in Hungary and Bulgaria crossed into Yugoslavia.

Tanks of PzRgt 36 (14. PzDiv) prior to the invasion of Yugoslavia. A PzKpfw IV Ausf E, fritted with 20mm *appliqué* armour, is parked in front of a *Tauchpanzer* IV Ausf E.

On 10 May 1940, Hitler ordered *Unternehmen* Marita to be initiated and 2.PzDiv, 9.PzDiv and 14.PzDiv departed from their holding areas in Bulgaria and advanced into Greece.

Below is an approximation of the number tanks deployed:

Tank strength as of 6 April 1941 5., 8. and 11. PzDiv Occupation of Yugoslavia		Tank strength as of 10 May 1941 2., 9. and 14. PzDiv Occupation of Greece	
Type	Number	Type	Number
PzKpfw I	9	PzKpfw I	9
PzKpfw II	134	PzKpfw II	126
PzKpfw 38(t)	125	PzKpfw III (3.7)	65
PzKpfw III (3.7)	44	PzKpfw III (5)	108
PzKpfw III (5)	58	PzKpfw IV	60
PzKpfw IV	62	PzBefWg	24
PzBefWg	19	StuG	approx 40
StuG	approx 40		

The figures confirm that the PzKpfw I was now considered to be obsolete and was no longer being issued to front-line units and the PzKpfw III was in the process of being up-gunned from the 3.7cm KwK L/45 to 5cm KwK L/42. Although a large number of PzKpfw IV are listed, there was not sufficient to equip each medium tank company with the planned (desired) 14 vehicles.

One of the few after-action reports to have survived was submitted by 1.Kp/PzRgt 33 on 9 April 1941:

According to the divisional order dated 5 April, the company was to be attached to advance party 'B' and move to the assembly near Kjustendil [Bulgaria]. The leader has ordered that it is to be formed as follows:

– Two PzKpfw II as the reconnaissance force
– 2.Zug [platoon] as the armoured spearhead (*Oberleutnant* Grüner).
– Engineer and rifle platoon in SdKfz 251, 3 minutes behind the rest of the company, supported by four PzKpfw IV (commanded by *Leutnant* Becker)
– A PzPiKp [armoured engineer company]
– A rifle company in armoured half-track vehicles
– A sIG company
– One 8.8cm FlaK battery
– One le Fh battery
– One 2cm FlaK platoon

8 April 1941

Our *Kradschützen* (motorcycle troops) have taken the heights northwest of Skopje, and the company will attack in the following order:

Oberleutnant Grüner (PzKpfw III)

Leutnant Grimm (PzKpfw IV)

Unteroffizier Pistrol (PzKpfw III)

Feldwebel Rüdiger (PzKpfw III)

Feldwebel Weber (PzKpfw II)

Despite attacks by enemy aircraft, the first 10km, which were over flat terrain, were quickly covered. On reaching the mountains, enemy mounted troops were encountered (possibly a rearguard). During the further advance the leading tanks successfully halted the destruction of an important bridge on the road to Kacanik. The enemy engineer was killed before igniting the explosive charge, allowing our *Panzerpioniere* to deactivate the charge. As we continued to advance, we observed the Luftwaffe attacking enemy positions around Kacanik. After negotiating numerous stone and wood street obstacles our leading formation entered Kacanik. The first three vehicles, as they rounded a sharp bend, were hit by a number of rounds fired from enemy 47mm anti-tank guns. The vehicles retreated under the cover of smoke provided by our PzKpfw IV. The other tanks engaged the enemy and successfully eliminated four anti-tank guns. During the advance through Kacanik, several hundred enemy troops surrendered, including a regimental commander and 14 officers.

The divisional symbol for 2.PzDiv is painted to the right of the *Balkenkreuz* – the name has nothing to do with the Balkans campaign, but refers to a cross made from two heavy (baulks) timbers. The vehicle chassis No.80383 has also been stencilled on the superstructure.

The crew of No.80383 has, possibly following orders, marked all tools and other attachments with the chassis number. The tank is in service with 2.PzDiv; note the spare running wheels attached to the rear of the turret.

The above appears to have been a 'textbook' commitment by using almost all the elements forming a tank division, including support services. The report also stated that the PzKpfw IV was highly-effective as a support for the tank; exactly as intended.

An after-action report from PzRgt 3 (2.PzDiv), which was deployed for *Unternehmen* Marita, highlights problems specific to armoured formations:

> After crossing the border, we spot the two crumbling houses and are fired at by Serbian infantry hiding in a thorn thicket. Our tanks, accompanied by infantry, advance south until we are stopped by a deep and wide anti-tank ditch and lines of reinforced concrete obstacles [Metaxas Line]. The lead vehicles come under fire from enemy machine gun and anti-tank gun positions. The other platoons try to go around the ditch but are stopped by mines; tank after tank is immobilized. The enemy is well concealed and cannot be targeted by our tanks.
>
> The 7.5cm [PzKpfw IV] platoon is positioned in the centre to support the attack. Our tanks continue to be halted by anti-tank mines. Our remaining tanks, FlaK guns and machine guns unleash a fierce barrage which allows our *Panzerpioniere* to succeed in clearing paths through minefield. Our '*Panzereierleger*' ['egg-laying tank'] – a PzKpfw I

Ladungsleger [demolition charge carrier] – are deployed to destroy the concrete anti-tank obstacles. Then our infantry advance and mop-up the last enemy infantry positions. The way is now clear, and our tank echelon can advance through the ditch towards Novo Selo, a village on the main road. Here our lead elements are heavily attacked, but only 1.Kp with two PzKpfw IV, the battalion staff including reconnaissance and engineer platoon manage to get through. No infantry are available as our advance has been too rapid.

The senior officers in the regiment made a vital error by assuming that the border would be poorly defended and therefore it was unnecessary to carry-out a full reconnaissance. If this had been done, the fortifications would have been assessed, and the minefields detected, resulting in fewer tanks being immobilized or destroyed. But the report does note the successful commitment of the *Ladungsleger* I.

After the campaign, *Armeeoberkommando* (AOK – army high command) 2 noted, on 9 May 1941, that all tracked vehicles had performed satisfactorily despite the difficult terrain.

But this was not entirely correct: many of the units had been deployed for the attacks on Poland and France; as a consequence, their vehicles were combat-worn and frequently suffered mechanical failures. After the end of the campaign, many units were returned to the Reich and re-equipped.

A crew member from a PzKpfw IV in service with PzRgt 33 (9.PzDiv), examines the drive sprocket and track for damage after striking a landmine. A pioneer, holding a mine detector, appears to have uncovered another mine.

When production of a new batch was ordered, many long-planned and often significant changes would be incorporated. From case to case, it was decided to retrofit some technical changes to already delivered vehicles. As far as possible, these changes were carried out by the workshop services of the Panzer division in the garrison or at the front.

These modifications were called *Formänderung* (change of shape) and were normally detailed in *Allgemeine Heeresmitteilungen* (AHM – army communications). On 7 December 1941, the strict ban on unauthorized *Formänderungen* to tanks was repeated:

> Contrary to the frequently repeated ban on unauthorized *Formänderungen*, the troops continue to add so-called 'improvements' to their equipment, which have not been ordered by the OKW. In one particular case, a Panzer division decided to reinforce the armour by welding a 15mm or 20mm thick plate on the front of their PzKpfw IV.
> If such work is not carried out at specialist assembly plant, there is no guarantee that the quality of the armour will be maintained. More importantly, practical tests have shown that unsuitable armour plate – some have tried iron plate – can lead to a reduction in ballistic resistance.

Between 1940 and 1941, the following orders were issued for improvements to be made on the PzKpfw IV:

- Installation of a '*Kurskreisel*' gyroscopic compass (November 1940).
- Modifications to the DKW generator unit for the electrically powered turret-traversing motor (January 1941).
- Installation of an improved carrier for towing cables (January 1940).

A PzKpfw IV Ausf D of PzRgt 8 (15. PzDiv) being loaded onto a cargo ship at Catania, Sicily. The rack, fabricated from wood, on the turret top was fitted to carry fuel cans. The tank has hot climate-type covers on engine compartment.

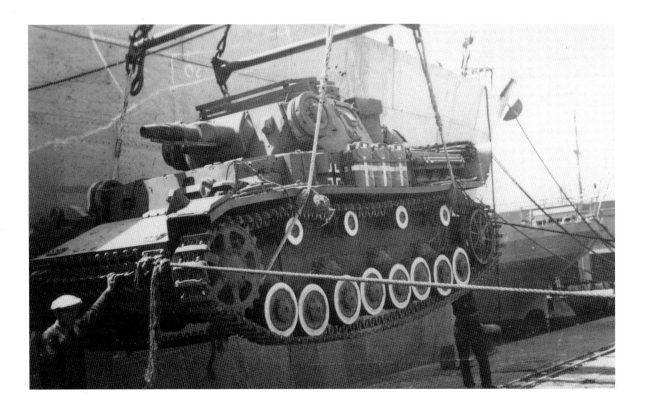

A PzKpfw IV Ausf E for PzRgt 8, being unloaded from a cargo ship in Tripoli. The thin tyres on the running wheels have been painted white to prevent damage from the heat of the desert sun. The three 'Jerrycans' marked with white crosses indicate that they are to be used only for water.

- Installation of new type of fuel nozzle for the starter of the Maybach HL 120 TRM (January 1940).
- Exchange of the magneto ignition for Maybach HL 120 (January 1940).
- Modified engine hatches with larger slits for cooling and combustion air (February 1940 but not implemented until 1941).
- Installation of new bearing bushes for the bevel gear (April 1940).
- Attachment of luggage box on the turret rear (April 1940).
- Installation of towing hook for a fuel trailer (June 1941).
- Replacement of the final drive hubs and bearings (July 1941).
- Mount a carrier for seven spare track links on the hull front (July 1941).
- Modification of the engine air supply ducting (August 1940).
- In November 1941 a list of compatible engines was published. Those used in the PzKpfw IV Ausf A to Ausf C and later Ausf C (from chassis No 80341) to Ausf F were interchangeable.

It is interesting to note that in the same period the PzKpfw III was subject to almost three times as many changes, a large number of which concerned the vulnerable Maybach Variorex gearbox.

The number of PzKpfw IV converted for hot climate conditions was relatively small, 30 PzKpfw IV Ausf D and ten PzKpfw IV Ausf E.

Interestingly, contemporary photographs show that the black 'tyres' on the running wheels and return rollers were coated with white paint.

Hitler, deeply concerned at the failure of the Italian campaign, decided to intervene and signed an order for 5.leDiv with PzRgt 5 and 15.PzDiv with PzRgt 8 to be sent to stabilize the situation in North Africa.

On 12 March 1941, the final tanks of 5.leDiv were landed at Tripoli and prepared for action. The force being assembled became known as the *Deutsche Afrika Korps* (DAK) and was commanded by the newly promoted

A *Zug* (platoon) for four PzKpfw IV halts for a short maintenance break. The black numeral '7' denotes 7.Kp. The tank carries a horizontal 'Wolfsangel' runic symbol and a triangle-shape divisional marking indicating that it is service with PzRgt 8 (15.PzDiv).

Tank strength: March to May 1941, 5. le and 15. PzDiv

Type	Number
PzKpfw I	25
PzKpfw II	90
PzKpfw III (5cm)	132
PzKpfw IV	37
PzBefWg	17

Generalleutnant Erwin Rommel. Almost immediately Rommel, in complete defiance of his orders, prepared a plan to attack British forces holding large areas of the Libyan desert. But these were a long distance from the coast and the ensuing march, much of which would be over difficult terrain, would test the mechanical reliability of not only his tanks but his entire motorized column.

The workshop company of PzRgt 5 issued the following report:

> The average marching distance of 700km in desert conditions had a very detrimental effect on the tanks. When we reached our holding positions near Tobruk, a number of the tanks, all with major engine problems (failures) and/or damaged running gear, had to be handed over to the two workshop companies:
>
> – 12 out of 25 PzKpfw I
> – Two out of Three kl PzBefWg
> – 19 out of 45 PzKpfw II
> – 44 out of 65 PzKpfw III
> – Six out of 17 PzKpfw IV
>
> A total of 83 tanks out of the 155 delivered to Tripoli. The cause of the excessive number of failures was the high speed required for the deployment and the difficult

A PzKpfw IV Ausf D of PzRgt 8 being driven up onto an SdAnh 116 flatbed trailer to be transported to distant battlefront. Once loaded the trailer would be hitched to an SdKfz 9 heavy half-track tractor.

terrain in the desert section in the vicinity of Trigh al Abd. But due to the situation the route, which was unsuitable for tanks, could not be avoided.

The engines in a number of tanks overheated and suffered a catastrophic failure due to running for long periods at high revolutions.

A PzKpfw IV being directed to a holding point. Any movement created a cloud of dust.

The clouds of dust generated by the column were another hazard which clogged the air filters on both tanks and other vehicles. German engineers quickly identified the problem; the engines in all types of vehicle were fitted with an oil-bath type air filter to prevent dust-laden air clogging the carburettor. German mechanics had worked on a number of captured British vehicles and found that most were fitted with a felt multi-layer filter. An urgent request was sent Germany for the supply of a similar type, and within a short time, they began to receive *Filzbalgfilter* (bellows-type filter).

The figures shown indicate that the PzKpfw IV was more mechanically reliable than the PzKpfw III.

Immediately after disembarkation in Tripoli, PzRgt 8 was ordered to a holding camp. Note the aperture for the ball-mounted machine gun has been covered and the extra fuel cans in the wooden rack on the turret. The distinctive symbol of the *Afrika Korps*, a palm tree and swastika, has been stencilled next to the driver's visor.

A PzKpfw IV Ausf D from
PzRgt 5: A few days after
arriving in Libya, the unit
took part in a military
parade through the streets
of the capital, Tripoli.

The high command of the DAK issued the following experience report:

5 le Div, 12 June 1941

Tactical experiences:

To date, all marching operations have taken place over clear and uncovered terrain
or on the only available major road (Via Balbia). Because of the large dust cloud
produced, our movements are easily observable by enemy reconnaissance aircraft.
Consequently, an active anti-aircraft defence must be incorporated within the
columns, and include 2cm FlaK (preferably on halftracks), and twin-mounted MG 34
on trucks. The distance between vehicles must be increased to 250m.
Maintaining the correct heading is only possible by using a standard marching
compass or the *Kurskreisel* (gyroscopic steering compass]. By day the British-issue
sun compass has proven to be very useful, although it has to be adjusted every 10
minutes and It can be used only in daytime.
Both the PzKpfw III and PzKpfw IV can each carry five additional water and fuel cans.
All drivers have been ordered to check there are sufficient water rations for the
crew since they already do this for fuel, oil and coolant. Also, they must be capable

of repairing simple faults or minor failures on their vehicle without calling on the services of a workshop. During hottest part of a day, it is advisable to halt the march, when possible, between 11:00hrs and 15:00hrs. This will help to lessen mechanical wear on our vehicles and reduce fatigue.

Combat

The Opponent: British troops, when in a defensive and always well-camouflaged position, will allow the attacker to approach until he is at close, and sometimes, very close range. The British soldier is tough in combat and more resolute than those from other nations we have so far fought against. An attack by our StuKa dive bombers appears to leave him unfazed, but when faced by a large force of German tanks he does not panic and makes a carefully considered retreat. On the other hand, British tank crews seem to have been instructed to avoid fighting our tanks, especially at distances below 300m: this also applies to the heavily armoured British Infantry Tank Mark II [Matilda]. Even after we break their line, the British stubbornly hold their positions on both sides of the breach, ready to close-off the enemy and fire on the flank of our attack. The British usually use their tanks for a counterattack. Here the infantry Mark IV [Churchill] and *Karetten* [Universal Carrier] can be attacked and defeated at all ranges.

A PzKpfw IV Ausf D from PzRgt 8: The desert battlefront often advanced so rapidly that the supply columns could not keep pace, which made it essential for the crew to make sure that they would have sufficient food and water for at least 24 hours.

Above: Three British Cruiser Tanks abandoned during *Unternehmen* Crusader (11 November to 30 December 1941). At the left is a Mark I CS (A9) armed with a Quick Firing 3.7-inch mountain howitzer: the others are Mark Is armed with the Ordnance Quick Firing 2 Pounder.

Right: A PzKpfw IV Ausf E of 8./PzRgt 5, the 20mm bolted-on armour plate has been blown off and the standard 30mm armour penetrated. The driver's visor has received a direct hit killing the driver, *Gefreiter* Herbert Probst. The chalked inscription shows the date as 13 December 1941.

The focus of our training must therefore be directed towards combating the British Mark II [Matilda]. Our most effective defensive weapons are the 5cm PaK anti-tank gun, the 5cm-armed PzKpfw III and the 7.5cm armed Pzkpfw IV firing armour-piercing and high-explosive ammunition (the latter seriously alarms British tank crews). To defeat a Mark II, our tanks must approach at top speed to a range of 200m, and then open fire.

Another effective weapon the British have is a 4cm anti-tank gun carried on a light truck [QF 2-pounder Portee].

Since the war in the desert was fought against an almost equally equipped opponent, German losses in the battle were considerable and replacements were limited. The invasion of the Soviet Union was imminent, and the OKW had already diverted substantial parts of the German *Wehrmacht* to fight in the east. This would result in the DAK without a sufficient supply of replacement tanks; a situation that could never be resolved since the only supply route was over the Mediterranean Ocean.

A portent of what was to come occurred in Naples during February 1941; the cargo ship *Leverkusen* was being loaded the tanks of PzRgt 5 when fire broke

PzRgt 5 used a large clearly-visible three-numeral turret number to identify its tanks. The fitting of track on the front plate, to give more protection, was strictly forbidden since if it became dislodged it could cause serious damage to the running rear and even immobilize the tank.

Tanks of PzRgt 8 on the way from Tripoli harbour to their holding area. The leading PzKpfw IV Ausf E has a complete set of add-on armour plates bolted to the front of the superstructure.

out and ten PzKpfw III and three PzKpfw IV were destroyed. The replacement vehicles were delivered to Tripoli in April 1941.

To compensate for the combat losses in April, a further 15 PzKpfw III and five PzKpfw IV were to be delivered on 4 June, followed by four PzKpfw II and six PzKpfw III on 30 June 1941. Four PzKpfw III were scheduled to be delivered on 10 July; but due to a lack of cargo ships these were not landed in Libya until August. The long delivery march from Tripoli would cause even more delays.

Most tank-versus-tank battles in the desert were fought at relatively long range, often over 500m. The terrain provided little or no cover, so any attacking formation quickly became a target for light and heavy artillery, or ground-attack aircraft.

Up until early 1942, most of the German tank crews in the DAK preferred the PzKpfw III when armed with 5cm KwK L/42, since the type was fast and agile, while the gun could defeat the front armour of most tanks in British service at long range. But not the Infantry Tank Mark I (Matilda II).

In contrast to the experiences in France, any PzKpfw IV armed with the 7.5cm KwK L/24 was regarded as only an effective support weapon in desert warfare. The gun had a low muzzle velocity which seriously affected accuracy at longer ranges, but the tank was deployed successfully as escort artillery.

German tank crews held another advantage, as the British did not have high-explosive ammunition for their tank guns.

German crews used both high-explosive and armour-piercing ammunition when fighting at close range, but accuracy was a always a problem. Most British tanks mounted a QF 2-pounder which could be deadly at close range.

The delivery of sufficient vehicles to replenish the two tank battalions in the division continued at a slow pace, and neither achieved full strength until the end of 1941.

Above: PzRgt 8 prepares for combat. The vastness of the North African desert allowed German tank units to operate in 'textbook' fashion, but such a large formation was vulnerable to enemy artillery and also easy to spot from the air.

Left: To troops fighting in desert conditions, regular hydration was as important to them as the supply of fuel and ammunition.

A PzKpfw IV Ausf D of 4./PzRgt 8 knocked out during *Unternehmen* Crusader. An early type *Nebelkurzenabwehrfvorrichtung* (NKAV – smoke grenade dispenser) is fitted on the engine exhaust silencer (muffler) – not a good position for a device containing explosive charges since the exhaust often glowed red-hot.

In early 1942 German *Luftflotte* 2, commanded by Albert Kesselring, had almost neutralized the Royal Air Force (RAF) bases on Malta. It was from this island that British aircraft launched attacks on German and Italian supply lines over the Mediterranean. This allowed the delivery of sufficient equipment to replenish the DAK in the first quarter of 1942.

Rommel was now confident that he could regain the initiative, and ordered his forces to advance on El Alamein, which they completed by June 1942.

Tank strength: May 1942, 15.PzDiv & 21.PzDiv	
PzKpfw II	58
PzKpfw III(k)	238
PzKPfw III(l)	18
PzKpfw IV	41
PzBefWg	8

But the resupply of his forces would remain critical. In March 1942, the OKW reported the loss of the Italian *Cuma* and the German *Achaia* cargo ships, both of which had been loaded with urgently needed fuel. Despite constant pressure from Rommel, a number of cargo ships, many loaded with fuel, would not sail because the Italian navy was unable to provide an escort.

Urgently needed replacement personnel remained in Italy: Hitler had ordered that ships carrying ammunition or fuel were not to be used for the transportation of troops. While at the same time, Mussolini forbade the use of passenger ships due to the extraordinary number of Italian ships sunk. Transfer by warship was not possible due to a serious shortage of heavy (furnace) oil.

The PzKpfw III (5cm KwK L/42) was the most numerous type to be deployed by the DAK, and a number of the new variant of the PzKpfw III Ausf M, armed with a more powerful 5cm KwK L/60, had already been delivered. The low number of PzKpfw IV in service, could be why the type was only deployed as a support tank in the desert.

When assessing forces available to *Panzerarmee Afrika*, it must remembered that they were supported by a significant Italian contingent. In addition to a number of infantry divisions, there were also two tank divisions, 'Ariete' and 'Littorio' in the desert, and a third 'Centauro' was being readied for transfer to Africa.

In May 1942, it was announced that the first shipment of 12 PzKpfw IV Ausf F 2, armed with the 7.5cm KwK L/43 and fitted for desert conditions was about to be delivered.

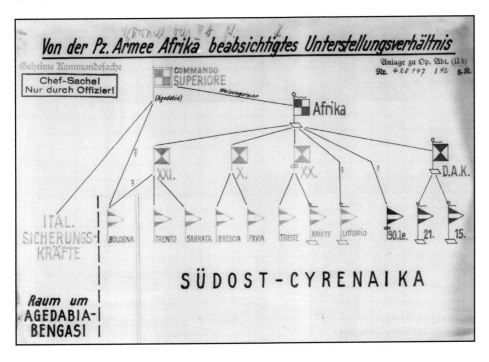

The *Kriegsgliederung* (order of battle) for *Panzerarmee Afrika* in early 1942, includes the German DAK and the three Italian army corps.

1941 – Barbarossa

Brimming with confidence at the success of his army, Adolf Hitler announced to the *Oberkommando der Wehrmacht* (OKW – high command of the armed forces), at a conference on 31 July 1940, that he had decided to invade the Soviet Union in 1941 and planning must begin immediately.

He envisaged a *Blitzkrieg*-type invasion – it is possible he was also aware that the German Reich would be not capable of fighting a prolonged war – and planned to eliminate Red Army opposition in the region with a series of armoured thrusts. His forces would then advance to Leningrad (25 August) and Moscow (reached on 26 November), and also occupy the Donets Basin to establish a frontline stretching from Archangelsk to Astrachan by the end of the year. Hitler was convinced that his mighty army could achieve another outstanding victory in just 17 to 22 weeks.

The German military build-up, along the borders of the Soviet Union, was achieved without attracting the attention of Russian (or British) intelligence services and by June 1941, three army groups – *Heeresgruppe Nord* (North), *Heeresgruppe Mitte* (Centre) and *Heeresgruppe Süd* (South) – and 17 Panzer divisions were ready for combat.

Changes in Production

After the French campaign, a programme was initiated to up-gun the PzKpfw III by mounting a 5cm KwK L/42 gun, whereas the PzKpfw IV was not subject to any fundamental modification or advancement apart from minor changes. But military planners, aware of the desperate shortages in the Reich, soon realized that the PzKpfw IV was not only economical to manufacture, but it was also a highly effective armoured fighting vehicle which could be upgraded to meet with the future demands of the *Panzertruppe*.

A large number of older *Ausführung* (Ausf – model or mark) of PzKpfw IV were deployed for the initial phase of *Unternehmen* Barbarossa. Here a PzKpw IV Ausf C, in service with 7.PzDiv, has been upgraded by fitting an antenna deflector, a Notek *Nachtmarschgerät* (night marching device) and also a carrier for spare track links.

A PzKpfw IV Ausf E ready for delivery from the Krupp-Grusonwerke factory in Magdeburg. From October 1940, all production tanks were to have 50mm thick bow plate, additional 30mm plate on the front of the superstructure and the armour for the sides of the hull increased to 20mm plates. But delivery problems often allowed only an incomplete implementation.

New PzKpfw IV were ordered in batches and these vehicles would have the latest *Formänderungen* (design changes) incorporated during production. Many of the changes could also be applied to earlier versions, but the work would be done by engineers in workshop units. An example was the fitting of a *Notek Nachtmarschgerät* (night driving) headlamp in February 1940.

As previously noted, any unauthorized modifications were strictly forbidden, but this was often ignored and most front-line units continued made changes to

Tank strength as of 22 June 1941, *Unternehmen* Barbarossa

PzKpfw I	152
PzKpfw II	743
PzKPfw 35(t)	155
PzKpfw 38(t)	394
PzKpfw III (3.7cm)	259
PzKpfw III (5cm)	707
PzKpfw IV	439
PzBefWg	167
StuG	200

suit their own requirements. The use of track links for added armour protection was also forbidden, but this too was ignored.

Interestingly, *Sturmartillerie* (assault artillery) units were allowed to make changes to their vehicles without seeking permission from a higher authority.

Technical Progress

This most important change was detailed in a bulletin sent from the OKW:

> *Kurskreisel-Anlage* (gyroscopic compass)…
> The installation of this item for the PzKpfw IV has to be performed only in accordance to the regulations as detailed in instruction D 659/1.

The compass was first fitted on new production lot (7./BW) which was designated PzKpfw IV Ausf F. Initially 128 units were ordered, but this would soon be increased to 500.

Although 50mm front armour had already been implemented on the Ausf E, that used on the Ausf F was face-hardened steel to further improve protection and the sides of hull were now 30mm thick.

Due to poor infrastructure, German forces the advancing into Soviet territory had to use major highways; the majority of secondary roads were little more than cart tracks. On many occasions a unit would be forced to proceed along a railway track, but these were often mined by retreating Red Army troops. As a precaution a member of the crew would walk ahead of the tank: here a PzKpfw IV Ausf D *Tauchpanzer* (diving tank), is looking for mines.

Above: The original specification, issued by the *Heereswaffenamt* (army weapons department) for the PzKpfw IV, also included the provision of an escape hatch for each member of the crew of five.

Right: Spring 1941: The leading PzKpfw IV Ausf D has been fitted with additional armour. But the following PzKpfw IV Ausf E has not been up-armoured.

Left: An unknown number of PzKpfw IV Ausf D were completed with the superstructure and turret of an Ausf E. Note the thin ring of sheet metal attached, possibly as a rain guard for the vision blocks, on the cupola.

Below: To improve the armour on the turret of a PzKpfw IV, add-on plating known as '*Vorpanzer*' was developed. Here a PzKpfw IV Ausf D of InfDiv 'Grossdeutschland' (with Ausf E drive sprockets), fitted with the armour and reinforced gun mantlet, is participating in a field exercise.

Above: The '*Vorpanzer*' was not introduced on a large scale, and most of the vehicles so fitted were used by the training units of the reserve army. This PzKpfw IV Ausf D is finished in *Dunkelgelb* (dark yellow) and was in service with a Holland-based unit in 1944.

Right: The '*Vorpanzer*' armour kit was extremely heavy and placed an uneven load on the turret ring which also affected the turret drive mechanism.

The shape of the superstructure was also altered: the face plate was now cut from a from single sheet of 50mm face-hardened steel. Other than this the entire superstructure was fabricated from 30mm steel plating. The turret was also improved: the front now had 50mm armour; the side and rear armour was increased to 30mm. Improvements were also made to the driver´s visor and to the ball mounting for the hull-mounted machine gun.

The increase in armour protection caused the weight to increase, which required changes to the running gear on the PzKpfw IV Ausf F: 40cm-wide tracks and therefore wider running wheels.

A total of 470 PzKpfw IV Ausf F were delivered between May 1941 and February 1942.

In the period before *Unternehmen* Barbarossa, a number of additional measures were ordered, since it was anticipated that marching distances would be significantly longer than those experienced during recent campaigns. It was decided that a small trailer to carry two 200-litre drums of fuel drums was to be produced to increase the cruising range of the PzKpfw IV. It was standard practice for the fuel to be transferred (a hand pump was fitted inside the tank) directly into the engine compartment while the vehicle was travelling. An unknown number *Betriebsstoff-Anhänger* (fuel trailers) were delivered.

From a report submitted by PzRgt 6 (3.PzDiv) on 27 December 1941:

What appears to be an undamaged PzKpfw IV Ausf D from 12.PzDiv has been loaded on an SdAnh 116, along with a VW Typ 82 *Kübelwagen* (bucket-seat car).

A PzKpfw IV Ausf E being reversed into the cover of a pine forest during training manoeuvres in preparation for *Unternehmen* Barbarossa on 22 June 1941.

The *Betriebsstoff-Anhänger* did not prove to be successful. The trailer can only be used during marches to an assembly area. The uncoupled trailers have to be collected, refilled and returned to the tanks. This was a difficult task due to the regiment not having enough vehicles to perform this task. This problem led to the loss of a large number of trailers, many of these having been 'borrowed' by other units.

The construction of the fuel trailer is too weak. Even during marches on good roads, drawbars and axles tended to break with much frequency. We consider the hand pump is unnecessary since the trailers were not be taken into combat. The tank should be refuelled before entering combat.

The regiment has no need for the *Betriebstoff-Anhänger*.

A column of PzKpfw IV from 11.PzDiv: note the distinctive sword-waving ghost symbol next to the official division sign; a white circle with a vertical bar.

Production

As a result of the campaigns in Poland and in France, the *Heereswaffenamt* (HWa – ordnance office) decided to increase production of the PzKpfw IV. (A similar decision was made 1938, but this never happened due to a lack of production capacity.) From 1938 to July 1941, the only company building the PzKpfw IV was Krupp-Grusonwerke at their facilities in Magdeburg-Buckau

Two tank commanders of 4.PzDiv are dressed in 1941-style *Sonderbekleidung für die Panzertruppe*, (special clothing for the armoured forces). By 1941, the distinctive black beret had been replaced by the *Schiffchen* (little boat) side cap.

which was working at full capacity. As a consequence, the HWa decided to issue contracts two other companies.

The manufacturer Vogtländische Maschinenfabrik AG (VOMAG) in Plauen, was a notable engineering company which designed and produced machinery, trucks and buses. A new facility needed to be built at Plauen and was to completed by late 1940; production was scheduled to commence in July 1941.

In Austria, only few companies with experience of producing armoured vehicles were available. As a result, it was decided in 1939 to build a

PzKpfw IV Ausf F

Weight:	23,674kg
Engine:	Maybach HL120 TRM
Performance:	265hp
Speed (maximum):	40km/h
Range (road):	210km
Range (cross country):	130km
Trench crossing:	2.3m
Fording depth:	80cm
Ground clearance:	40cm

completely new tank plant, code named '*Spielwarenfabrik*' (toy factory), in St Valentin. The facility now known as Nibelungenwerk, began producing the PzKpfw IV in November 1941.

Some 30 had been delivered each month by the end of June 1941, but month-by-month the output continued to improve.

Improving Firepower

In the summer of 1941, the 7.5cm *Kopfgranate* rot (Pz) (KGr – armour-piercing round) was the only, and inadequate, ammunition available to fire at enemy armour: maximum penetration was 41mm at 100m range, and 35mm at a range of 1,000m. Due to the 7.5cm Kwk l/24 having a low muzzle velocity, the HWa decided that the development of more effective types of armour-piercing round would be an unnecessary waste of resources..

Due to the fact that the gun was initially intended to be used in the artillery manner, muzzle velocity was relatively low, resulting in poor accuracy. The gunners had to rely on bracketing.

This 7.5cm KwK L/24 was never intended for tank-versus-tank combat, being originally designed for the infantry support role. But the reality of battle would make military planners change their thinking, especially after the first months of *Unternehmen* Barbarossa.

The unexpected appearance of the Soviet-built T-34 medium tank and KV-1 heavy tank would mark the sudden end of the all-conquering German tank; all types, all including the PzKpfw IV, proved to be far inferior to the well-armoured and mobile Red Army tanks.

PzKpfw IV production 1941		
	Production	Total Stock (including bridge-layer tanks)
January	31	419
February	26	453
March	28	476
April	36	459
May	29	499
June	38	517
July	38	531
August	44	488
September	46	470
October	51	499
November	52	485
December	61	511

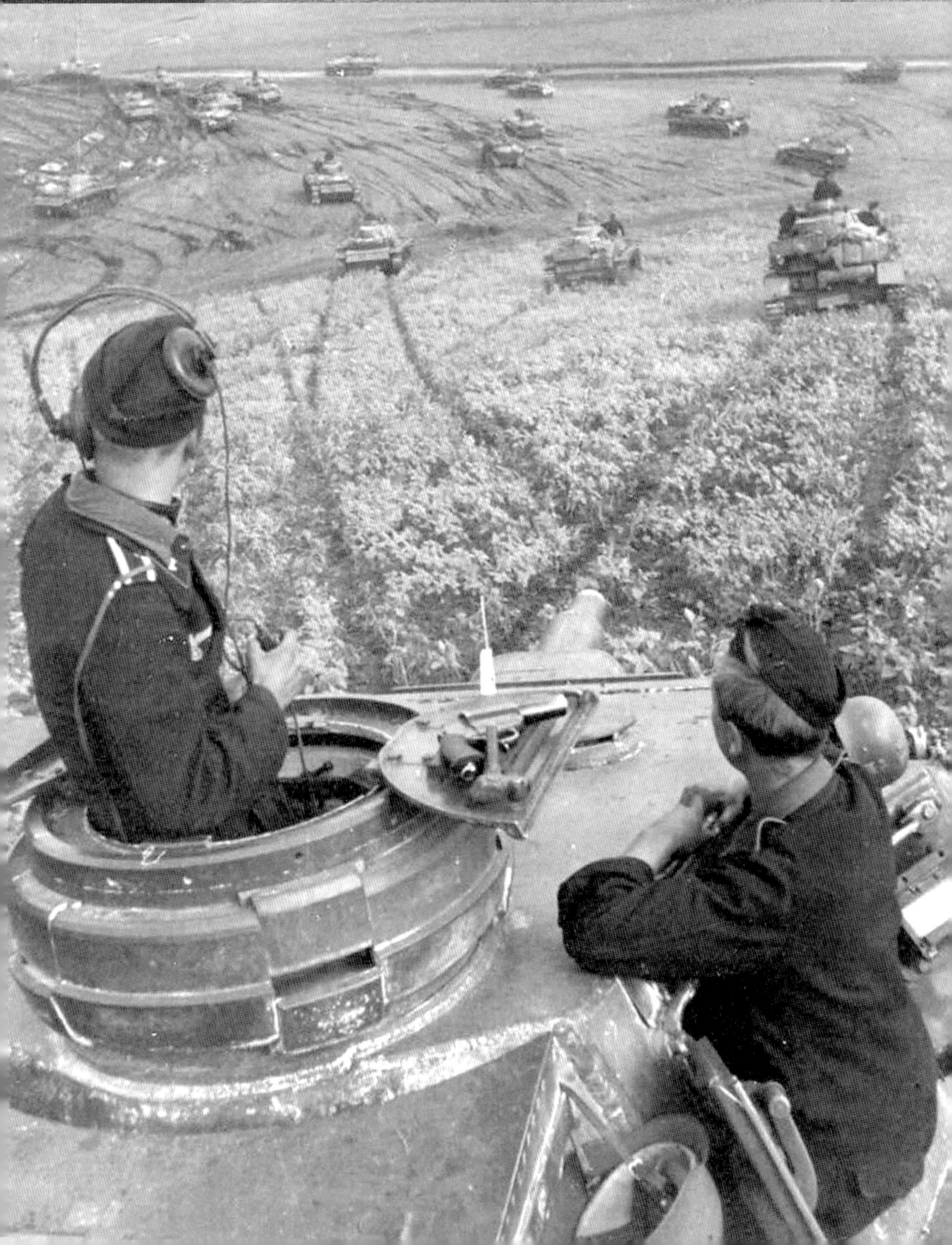

Far left: March 1942: The commander of a PzKpfw IV Ausf F battalion observes the advance of his tanks. Note the *Leuchtpistole* (flare gun) laying on the hatch lid.

Left: A PzKpfw IV Ausf E of PzRgt 7 (10.PzDiv) being repaired by men from the *Werkstatt-Kompanie* (workshop company). The tank is marked with a large numeral '8' to indicate that it is from 8.Kp. The bison symbol of a PzRgt is almost hidden by the large fascine.

Infantrymen ride to their next battle on a PzKpfw IV in service with 20.PzDiv. The tank has been fitted with a spare track carrier on the transmission cover. Note the radio operator/hull machine gunner wears overalls instead of the standard black uniform.

For German tank crews and anti-tank gunners the situation was disturbingly simple; had the so far victorious *Panzerwaffe* finally met its match?

The T-34 was a revolutionary design: the front and sides of the superstructure were fabricated from 45mm armour plate sloped at 45 degrees. The vehicle was fitted with wide tracks and running gear purposely designed for operating, in all conditions, over typical Russian terrain. A powerful diesel engine allowed the vehicle to have a top speed of 35kph.

The KV-1 was a more conventional design of heavy tank and was heavily armoured by 1941 standards. For simplicity the type was fitted with same engine and transmission as that used for the T-34.

The German approach to remedy the threat posed by the latest Soviet tanks was threefold:

a) Immediate provision of means for existing tanks to cope with the superior Soviet tanks.
b) Quickest possible introduction of high-performance guns for all available tank types to restore an equality of arms.
c) Question whether it had been really necessary to cancel all armour related development projects, while expediting the design of modern tanks to establish a lasting superiority.

A PzKpfw IV Ausf E with a damaged suspension being transported to a workshop. The SdAnh 116 is being towed by an SdKfz 8 heavy half-track tractor; a second driver steered the rear wheels from the small cab.

Item c.) would later lead to the production of the PzKpfw V Panther and PzKpfw VI Tiger. Item b.) would lead to the introduction of the high-velocity *Langrohr* (lang – long barrelled) 5cm and 7.5cm tank guns.

For German forces struggling on the *Ostfront* (East front) any quick solution would have been appreciated. Although improved tactics, improved signals equipment and procedures assisted German forces in making a rapid advance on Moscow, the Panzer divisions desperately waited to be provided with more powerful weapons.

Dust, whether on the dry Russian steppe or in the arid deserts of North Africa, caused serious mechanical problems. The Maybach engines were fitted with oil bath-type air filters which easily and frequently became clogged.

PzKpfw IV, T-34 and KV-1, 1941

	PzKpf IV Ausf F	T-34 M 1941	KV-1 M 1940
Main armament:	7.5cm L/24	76.2mm L/41	76.2mm L/41
Armour (maximum):	50mm (at front only)	45mm (slanted all round)	75mm (all round)
Armour penetration: (500m)	41mm	75mm	75mm
Weight:	22,2660kg	26,720kg	44,200kg
Performance:	265hp (petrol)	500hp (diesel)	550hp (diesel)
Speed (maximum):	40kph	53kph	35kph
Range (road):	210km	455km	335km
Range (cross country):	130km	200km	130km
Fording depth:	80cm	145cm	145cm
Ground clearance:	40cm	52cm	52cm

Above: A column of tanks from 20.PzDiv advance along a dusty road during the summer of 1941. The crews have placed a Swastika flag on top of the turret to avoid being attacked by *Luftwaffe* aircraft.

Right: A *Tauchpanzer* IV (Ausf E) has the skull over water badge of PzRgt 18 and the divisional symbol for 18.PzDiv on the turret stowage box. Note the damaged running wheel and the replacements.

Hartkern and *Hohlladung*

In 1941, the 3.7cm KwK and 5cm KwK L/42 standard tank guns mainly fired high-explosive shells to fight enemy tanks, but several different types of anti-tank ammunition were available:

The *Panzergranat-Patronen* (PzGrPatr – armour-piercing shell) was supplied as the 3.7cm PzGrPatr and 5cm PzGrPatr for all models of the PzKpfw III.

A new type was produced for the 5cm tank gun; the 5cm PzGrPatr 39 was an APC (armour-piercing capped) round which had much-improved penetration performance.

Development of an HVAP (high-velocity armour-piercing) round was completed in 1940. The type was designated *Panzergranat-Patrone* (PzGrPatr) 40 and had a core of high-density *Hartkern* (tungsten carbide) inside a shell cast from softer metal, normally an alloy. Consequently, it was 50 percent lighter than the PzGrPatr 39, which resulted in a significant improvement in muzzle velocity and thus much better penetration. But, though the maximum effective range of the 5cm PzGrPatr 40 was lower than that of the PzGrPatr 39, it was still effective at up to 500m.

The ever-present shortage of tungsten meant that it was impossible for ammunition manufacturers to maintain a sufficient supply of PzGrPatr 40 rounds. Despite restrictions, the PzGrPatr 40 was developed so that it was suitable for all German anti-tank and tank guns; the only exception was the 7.5cm KwK L/24 of the PzKpfw IV.

A PzKpfw IV Ausf E appears to be carrying an unusually large amount of heavy chain. Like many others in Russia, the tank carries heavy wooden beams on the side of the superstructure. These would be for the recovery of a bogged-down tank.

To improve the anti-tank capabilities of the 7.5cm KwK L/24 gun, shaped-charge (Munroe effect) technology was revisited. *Hohlladung* (hollow charge) ammunition had been introduced before the war and was used in France to destroy the bunkers in the Maginot line.

The same technology was used to design a standard type of ammunition. On 22 December 1941, Hitler issued an order from his office announcing that new technology, 7.5cm GrPatr 38, was approved and production was to begin immediately. To identify it as a hollow-charge type an (Hl) suffix was used.

At first performance was found to be very bad, and almost equal to a standard armour-piercing round. Then a change to the shape of the hollow charge led to an improvement in performance. The new version was identified as the Hl/B and it seems logical that the first production version was re-designated Hl/A.

Documents from early 1942 list two types as being produced: Hl/A which could penetrate 70mm thick armour ;whereas the Hl/B could penetrate 75mm.

The same document also notes that the 7.5cm KGr rot (Pz) was taken out of production, but somewhat confusingly, a document dated December 1944 shows that it was still available.

It has proved to be impossible to uncover any after-action reports detailing the performance of hollow-charge ammunition fired from the 7.5cm KwK L/24 gun mounted in PzKpfw IV. But a report sent by *Sturmgeschütz-Batterie* (StuGBttr – assault gun battery) 667 does provide some interesting detail, since the PzKpfw IV Ausf A to Aus F and the StuG Ausf A to Ausf F mounted

A PzKpfw IV Ausf F parked next to a PzKpfw III Ausf G mounting a 5cm KwK L/42. The turret number denotes the tank as that of the commander of 4.Kp of I.Abt.

the same 7.5cm gun, but known as the *Sturmkanone* (StuK – assault gun) in the StuG.

An after-action report of StuGBttr 667 dated January 1942 stated:

During the defensive battles at Pogostje between 18 January and 20 January two *Sturmgeschütze* of our battery have destroyed the following tanks using the newly issued hollow-charge ammunition:

Four KV-1 tanks
Five T-34 tanks
One medium tank [not specified]

We experienced the following:

1) Since the 7.5cm GrPatr 38 has no tracer, we used PzGr rot to bracket a target. After the first hit we then fired GrPatr 38 (Hl).

2) We experienced only a very few ricochets, even on sloping armour; it simply sticks to the surface and then penetrates. The process resembles a mechanic using a welding torch. The tank would then catch fire and become enveloped by thick smoke.

3) Precise examination of a hit was not possible since all the burnt-out tanks remained in enemy territory.

A PzKpfw IV Ausf D, from 19.PzDiv, towing the small fuel trailer which was issued to tank units at the beginning of *Unternehmen* Barbarossa. The tanks of 19.PzDiv can be identified by the unit-built stowage box fitted on the rear of the turret, and the spare track links and running wheels carried in racks on the trackguard.

Above: The workshop company was able to carry out even major repairs in the field. The engineers have erected a portable lifting gantry to remove the engine from a PzKpfw IV. A replacement Maybach HL 120 TRM is ready to be fitted.

Right: Early production models of the PzKpfw IV were not fitted with carriers for replacement running wheels and track links. These would be fabricated and fitted by field engineers.

4) We fired at ranges from 100m to 600m with equally good results.

5) The fuse is very susceptible, even a thin branch would cause a detonation. None of our shells failed. (important for secrecy)

6) The GrPatr 38 (Hl) has similar ballistic characteristics to the GrPatr 34 [high explosive], but has a longer range than the *Panzergranate* [PzGr rot Pz]. After bracketing a target with *Panzergranate* at a range of 600m to 1,000m it is essential to re-adjust the gunsight by 100m before switching to GrPatr 38 (Hl).

The report praises the performance of the new ammunition, which would continue to be used, with much success, by German anti-tank and tank force. The 7.5cm GrPatr 38 (Hl) could obviously defeat all modern Soviet tanks at ranges of 1,000m.

But a PzKpfw IV could be destroyed at an even longer range by the Russian 76.2mm L/41.5 tank gun.

The introduction of 3.7cm and 5cm PzGr 40 ammunition for the PzKpfw III significantly increased the combat value of the tank. But German authorities were desperate to keep the technology hidden from the British. The current anti-tank gun in service was the Ordnance Quick-Firing 2-pounder: although light by German standards, it was accurate at close range, but HVAP ammunition was never produced for the gun. The British concentrated their effort on completing development of the Ordnance QF 6 Pounder which was scheduled to enter service in April 1942.

In autumn 1941, the HWa ordered that all new production tanks (PzKpfw III and IV) must be fitted with *Vorpanzer* (spaced armour). This designation is however misleading since all previous add-on armour could be named like this; some sources call spaced armour '*Schottpanzer*'. The first to be fitted were the PzKpfw III Ausf L which had an extra 20mm armour riveted to the 50mm front plate of the superstructure.

German tank guns 1941, armour penetration

Ordnance	Calibre length	Type of ammunition	Type	Vo mps	Penetration 100m	500m	1,000m	1,500m
3.7cm KwK	L/45	3.7cm PzGr	AP	745	35	29	22	20
		3.7cm PzGr 40	APCR	1020	64	31	-	-
5cm KwK	L/42	5cm PzGr	AP	685	53	43	32	24
		5cm PzGr 39	APC	685	55	47	37	28
		5cm PzGr 40	APCR	1050	94	55	-	-
7.5cm KwK	L/24	7.5cm Gr rot Pz	AP	385	41	38	35	32
		7.5cm GrPatr HL/A	HVAP	450	70	70	70	70

The onset of winter in Russia would cause many problems for German tank troops. Since military commanders had expected a quick victory, they now found that they lacked the means to fight in the harsh winter conditions of the *Ostfront* (East front). For example, troops did not have winter clothing and engineers did not have lubricants and other essentials suitable for the cold.

For the PzKpfw IV a similar solution was developed, but the turret was reinforced by welding on 20mm plating. A curved armoured plate was bolted to the gun mantlet and the front plate on the superstructure was also fitted with spaced armour.

Contemporary photographs of mainly PzKpfw IV Ausf D and E, and a few Ausf F, were thus modified. First deliveries took place by early 1942; no further detail is known.

From early 1942 an organic increase of frontal armour protection of the PzKPfw IV production was decided, but the overall number of vehicles fitted with *Vorpanzer* was low. Most photos seem to show them being used by *Ersatz- und Ausbildungs-Abteilungen* (training and replacement units).

At the beginning of the Russian campaign the vast majority of after-action or experience reports from tank regiments down to company level did not differentiate between their PzKpfw III and PzKpfw VI. Possibly they felt it unnecessary because the majority of Russian tanks being encountered were poorly armoured T-26 and BT, which were easily defeated by all tank guns, including 2cm and 3.7cm KwK.

From an after-action report submitted by PzRgt 6 on 23 July 1941:

Report on the deployment of 8 *Kompanie* [8.Kp] near Mogilev on 12 July 1941:

The 8.Kp was held by II.Abt as a reserve near the tank track. In the course of the attack by Battalion Wellmann, which 7.Kp had been sent to assist, requested tank support. When questioned, they reported that 7.Kp had failed to connect. Following orders from the commander of II.Abt, 8.Kp moved to the right of the tank track to Mogilev to make contact with Wellmann. At Buimitshi the company joined the rifle company and engaged in a fight against enemy anti-tank guns. The 7.5cm high-explosive fire quickly silenced all guns. During the march back we got the impression that Battalion Wellmann was completely torn apart and there was no connection to the individual

A PzKpfw IV Ausf E from 20.PzDiv, being camouflaged with a water-soluble chalk or lime-based whitewash paint.

companies. Immediately on arriving at the *Abteilungs Gefechtsstand* (battalion command post) in Sselez, 8.Kp received orders to attack to the left of the tank track in order to join 5.Kp. The company attacked in *Breitkeil* (inverted wedge formation) between the railway and tank track and after a few hundred metres the enemy opened fire from well-concealed positions in the yard of a brickworks and on the edge of woodland to the west of Mogilev. Nevertheless, the company continued to attack until the first target was taken, after which enemy fire for became weaker the first time. The PzKpfw IV commanded by *Leutnant* Niemabers received a hit on the turret which wounded the gunner and locked the traverse. Suddenly, 8.Kp began receiving urgent radio calls from 5.Kp. The battalion quickly gave us orders to assist 5.Kp, and we immediately turned left to the railway embankment. Directly in front of the embankment tank No.800, commanded by *Leutnant* Köhler, the *Kompanieführer* [company commander], ran over a mine, damaging the hull and destroying the running gear. The driver *Obergefreiter* Büchler was severely wounded. A PzKpfw II called in to recover the wounded man also a hit mine, which only damaged the running gear. *Leutnant* Jacob took command of the company. In the attempt to recover the injured driver, the entire crew of No.800 was wounded by machine gun fire. Now the company formed a 'hedgehog' defensive formation around the No.800 and fired on the enemy resistance machine-gun nests positioned on the edge of the town. A few tanks advanced up to a covered tank obstacle [ditch] and forced the Russians to retreat. The company destroyed two armoured cars and two anti-tank guns.

Soon afterwards the company received orders by radio to withdraw, taking all wounded men with them. Three tanks moved up to recover the many wounded of the rifle company. During the return drive a PzKpfw IV hit a mine, although all three tanks were using the same track, which slightly damaged the running gear. Another tank, which was reversing away, also hit a mine and was immobilized. Despite heavy machine-gun and artillery fire the company tried, for more than an hour, to get both tanks moving again, but the attempt failed. The company decided to drive back with some 80 PoWs, leaving two men behind to guard the tanks until our heavy half-track vehicles were available to recover them.

The regimental staff made a statement which suggested that the attack was unsuccessful due to the difficult terrain. The railway embankment, covered by enemy anti-tank guns supported by artillery, was an obstacle that could not be overcome without supporting artillery fire or an attack by the *Luftwaffe*. The action cost the 8.Kp a total loss as well as two disabled PzKpfw IV and some severely wounded personnel.

The workshop company added some further notes:

Above: Although these PzKpfw IV Ausf F appear to blend in with the terrain, the standard black uniform is conspicuous against the white winter scene. This was resolved in winter 1942 when tank crews were issued with a reversible camouflaged uniform.

Left: A PzKpfw IV Ausf F carries two spare running wheels in a carrier fabricated and fitted by field engineers. In mid-1942, these became a standard fit when the PzKpfw IV Ausf G entered production.

The German military preferred to use railway transport to move tanks over a long distance to avoid damaging the running gear and, particularly, the problematic *Seitenvorgelage* (final-drive units). The vehicles are loaded on SSys *schwere Plattformwagen* (heavy flat car). Each of the ammunition boxes stacked on the engine deck hold two 7.5cm high-explosive rounds.

A PzKpfw IV Ausf D from PzRgt 15 (11.PzDiv) being retrieved from a muddy river bank. If the heavy recovery section equipped with half-track tractors was not available, a tank would have to be used. Officially this procedure was strictly prohibited in order to protect the delicate gearing in the final-drive units.

Equipment situation

PzRgt 6 entered combat with 208 tanks including a number of command tanks. As of July 1941, we have lost 54 tanks due to enemy action and two by a shortage of spare parts. At the moment there are some 40 tanks in the workshop, with engine problems, which cannot be repaired because of a shortage of cylinder-block liners. Initially there had been a shortage of rubber-banded running wheels. We expect a larger number of damaged tracks in the near future, especially on the PzKpfw IV.

Since the regiment held a relatively high stock of spare parts most of the repairs could be completed relatively smoothly. With the exception of three exchange HL 120 TRM engines, a manual gearbox for a PzKpfw IV and some spare parts for PzKpfw II, all parts were readily available.

In contrast to the deployment in the west, the large amount of dust generated in Russia caused disproportionately more engine damage. Almost all engine wear can be attributed to dust accumulation. This could have been reduced by carefully cleaning the air filters and changing the engine oil frequently. The regiment has been in uninterrupted combat for four weeks, so that too little time could be made available for this maintenance work. The mileage of the engines could have been increased by about 300km to 500km with appropriate care. The mileage in service of each PzKpfw totalled 1,100km to 1,500km. Damage to the running gear can be described as normal.

According to the document PzRgt 6 had 17 PzKpfw III 'b' and five PzKpfw II in its le PzKp (to KStN 1171 [Sd]). The regiment had a complement of

100 tank personnel and 82 and in the service echelon. The letter 'b' was an unofficial identifier for tanks armed with the 5cm KwK L/42: those armed with the 3.7cm KwK had the letter 'a'. The m PzKp was issued with ten PzKpfw IV plus five PzKpfw II (to KStN 1175), 65 tank personnel and 79 in the service echelon.

In November 1941, *Oberleutnant* Richter submitted a report which included a list of suggested improvements:

> At the moment the regiment does not have any weapons able to penetrate the new enemy tanks [T-34 and KV-1]. In terms of leadership our tanks are still far superior, thanks to being fitted with radio equipment.
>
> Improvements to the PzKpfw IV:
> – Running wheels are too small.
> – Spring blocks too weak, swing arm bearings wear out too frequently, the spring-retaining bolts often fall out.
> – The problem with the final-drive units continue, the transverse driveshafts often fail.
> – The new version [Ausf F] is too heavy and the engine lacks power.
> – Brackets must be fitted to carry spare rollers and track links. Also we need a stowage bin.
> – Larger fuel tanks must be installed (fuel cans are dangerous).
> – The diversity of types makes the supply of spare parts more difficult. There are four different types (Ausf B to Ausf F) in a company.
> – The anti-armour performance of the 7.5cm KwK is far too low. The announced delivery of special ammunition [GrPatr 38] is still awaited.
> – Ammunition racks for more rounds have to be installed. We carry 120 instead of 80 shells; the extra 40 have to be stacked behind the driver.
> – The opening in the *Panzerführerkuppel* (commander's cupola) is too narrow. It is not possible to enter when wearing a heavy overcoat.
> – Company and platoon leaders must be provided with a rangefinder. Brackets must be installed in each tank to carry a replacement in case of a failure.

The list is written by an officer in the combat troop, who most probably had no engineering training or experience. Many of his complaints are understandable, but any radical changes would be impossible to incorporate. The indication that the current Ausf F is too heavy or underpowered seems very amateurish, but his request for an integrated rangefinder is very prescient. However, this item would not become standard equipment, even for the PzKpfw V Panther and PzKpfw VI Tiger, until later in the war.

Although fitted with *Winterketten* (winter tracks) this PzKpfw IV Ausf C has skidded off a road and become stuck in a gully.

The arrival of the Russian winter would bring a significant number of losses. German tanks and other vehicles had not been designed to operate in almost 'arctic' conditions.

PzRgt 33 (9.PzDiv) was one unit to be badly affected:

Damage caused by extremely low temperatures:
Most damage is caused by the lack of a good winter oil for engines and transmissions. The engines will not easily turn over in very cold conditions, and this causes a lot of wear and tear on the electric-powered starter. The substitute inertia starter is difficult to use. When an open fire is lit under the hull to heat the engine, electrical cables, auxiliary-drive belts and water hoses are often burnt. The drive shaft on the oil pump often fractures due to the oil lacking viscoscity. At temperatures below -15 degrees centigrade, turrets often seize solid because condensation collects behind and under the ring and freezes; fine snow can cause the same problem. All optics that are not lubricated with cold-resistant grease fail at temperatures below -15 degrees centigrade.

In February 1942 PzRgt 33 (9.PzDiv) answered the previously mentioned questionnaire for tank regiments. For the PzKpfw IV:

The PzKpfw IV proved to be generally useful.

– The new 7.5cm special ammunition [7.5cm GrPatr 38 Hl] proved itself in combat against T-34 and KV-1.

– The ammunition equipment of the PzKpfw IV should consist of 70 percent high explosive, 20 percent armour piercing and 10 percent smoke.

– A direct hit from Soviet 7.62cm guns quickly leads to fire inside the PzKpfw IV. Often the ammunition explodes and completely destroys the tank.

– The ammunition cartridge cases delivered by our supply services are often corroded.

– The *Fliegerbeschuss-Gerät* [anti-aircraft mount] 41 for the turret MG 34 did not prove successful. During bombing attacks the crews were ordered into their tanks.

– In very hot weather, drivers of the Pzkpfw III and IV had were strictly instructed to drive slowly, because the rubber-banded running wheels shredded after a short time.

The workshop company has removed the tracks from this damaged PzKpfw IV and stacked them on the engine cover. The tank has been attached to an SdKfz 9 heavy half-track tractor ready to be towed away for repair.

The beginning of the year marked the first setbacks for Hitler's plans. The German offensive in the east was stalled at the gates of Moscow. In North Africa, Rommel's advance had been pushed back as a consequence of *Unternehmen* Crusader.

During the early stages of the war, commonly referred to as the *Blitzkrieg*, the German armoured vehicles had proven spectacularly effective tools with which to enact the German idea of armoured warfare. However, from the beginning of the invasion of Russia, the PzKpfw IV (*Begleitwagen*), had to perform tasks the tank was not designed for. As this problem was foreseen, several measures had already been implemented to adapt the tank, including increasing armour protection and the introduction of *Hohlladungs-Geschosse* (shaped-charge ammunition), which was available in greater numbers by the beginning of 1942.

The introduction of *Hohlladungs-Geschosse* could alleviate the critical situation on the Eastern Front but only to a certain degree. Combat against T-34 and KV was now possible at ranges up to 1,000m. By taking advantage of the Russian tank's limited observation means, the inadequate provision of radios and the Russian soldiers' tactical deficiencies, many tank battles could be decided. In the patchwork structure of northern Russia those battles often took place at relatively short ranges, where the PzKpfw III and PzKpfw IV could play to their strengths.

However, the steppe in southern Russia and the vast expanse of the North African battlefield had some characteristics in common. While being ideal for operations of large-scale armoured units, many battles were fought at longer ranges, which brought new problems.

By early 1942, the Russian 76.2mm F-34 tank gun predominated on the Eastern Front. It could engage all German tanks including the PzKpfw IV well

A PzKpfw IV Ausf H, armed with a 7.5cm KwK 40 L/48, was able to defeat any enemy armour, including the KV-85 heavy tank in service with the Red Army. But in late 1944, the tank was clearly outgunned when the Soviet-built 85mm D-5T, the US-built 76mm M1A1 and the British Ordnance Quick Firing (OQF) 17-pounder (mounted in the Sherman IIC Firefly) entered the battle. (Getty)

When the PzKpfw IV Ausf F was armed with a 7.5cm KwK 40 L/43, the German *Panzertruppe* had a tank capable of defeating a T-34 and were able to confidently continue their advance on the Caucasus.

outside the German armour's own range. The Germans were however able to adapt their tactics by calling in heavy artillery and FlaK; and in addition, at that time the Luftwaffe enjoyed air superiority.

While being less urgent, the situation in North Africa was comparable at the turn of the year. With the unexpected deployment of the US-built M3 medium tank in May 1942, the British had also a weapon able to engage German armour beyond the effective range of their own weapons.

By autumn 1941 it had become clear that only the introduction of a high-velocity gun could remedy this problem. This of course had been well known to the *Waffenamt* engineers for years. Consequently, the work on such a solution for both *Panzertruppe* and *Sturmartillerie* had begun early.

The development of a new weapon, its thorough testing and preparation for production, of course takes time. While engineers generally deal with the technical implementation only, the officials of the *Heereswaffenamt* (HWa – army ordnance office) had the duty of implementing these ideas and coordinating them with the logistical and material realities. A good example is the rearmament of the PzKpfw III, whose production line was changed in 1940 to the new 5cm KwK L/42. At the same time the 5cm PaK 38 L/60, the

new weapon of the tank destroyers, was to be introduced. When compared to the L/42 gun, this weapon showed a 30 percent higher penetration rate when firing the PzGrPatr 39, and this advantage increased to 40 percent when using the PzGr 40 (at distances below 1,000m). Despite these obvious advantages, in 1940 the opportunity was missed to install this valuable and powerful weapon in the PzKpfw III, the main carrier of tank vs tank combat. This decision prevented the tank from being equipped with a weapon that would have reduced its inferiority to the T-34 and KW in 1941 (its strongest tank opponents).

Krupp had in fact started work on a long-barrelled 7.5cm gun before the outbreak of war. This L/41 ordnance was installed and test-fired in a modified *Sturmgeschütz* by May 1940. These trials revealed a gun with numerous design flaws, but why this interesting pre-war approach was not followed up is unknown. Reluctance to make a potentially costly wrong decision and time and energy-sapping conflicts of opinion surely contributed.

By February 1941 Hitler's bureau had ordered the 5cm PaK 38 high velocity anti-tank gun installed into the turret of both the PzKpfw III and IV. While this was initially deemed impossible for the PzKpfw III, a 5cm L/60

A newly delivered PzKpfw IV Ausf F issued to a training and replacement unit. A PzKpfw I driver training vehicle is parked in the background.

gun was modified and fitted to the turret of a PzKpfw IV Ausf D. Photos show this vehicle being tested in Tyrol by January 1942. Production did not commence, possibly because the long-barrelled 7.5cm ordnance promising far better performance was already under development. After ironing out some technical problems, the 5cm KwK L/60 was installed in the PzKPfw III's turret instead.

By November 1941 the *Waffenamt* (ordnance office) recorded adoption of the new 7.5cm PaK L/46 in the turret of the PzKpfw IV. Initially called PaK 44, this weapon should have entered production as the 7.5cm PaK 40 by April 1942. But the weapon's long cartridge (716mm) prevented installation in the PzKpfw IV turret. For this reason, the rifled Rheinmetall PaK 44 barrel was combined with the breech of the Krupp L/41 gun, which used thicker but shorter cartridges (495mm) designed for installation in an armoured superstructure with restricted space.

Analogous to the PaK 44, the new weapon was called KwK 44. The development sheet quotes the calibre length with L/43, and later an L/48 barrel would follow. This was to simplify production; the early L/43 barrel showed an irregular angle of twist ranging from 6 degrees to 9 degrees; the longer barrel had a continuous angle of 7 degrees.

Far left: In 1941, a 5cm KwK 39 L/60 was mounted in the turret of a PzKpfw IV, but after a series of firing trials the idea was dropped in favour of the much more powerful 7.5cm KwK 40 L/48.

Far left bottom: After the problems with the cartridge chamber and the ammunition had been solved, the 7.5cm KwK 40 L/48 was cleared for mounting on the PzKpfw IV Ausf F.

Left: New tanks were delivered from the manufacturer to *Heereszeugämter* (HZA – army depots), where further equipment would be fitted. The chalked letter 'F' indicates that the vehicle has been cleared for delivery to a tank unit.

Engineers working to replace a suspension bogey on a PzKpfw IV Ausf G after the tank had struck a mine laid by retreating enemy infantry.

Although Adolf Hitler showed a keen interest in weaponry, he had a tendency to meddle and often overruled decisions made by his 'experts'. Here the Führer, and his large entourage, inspects PzKpfw IV Ausf G during a visit to the Nibelungenwerke in St Valentin. Note, the muzzle brake is incorrectly fitted.

The KwK 44, now renamed to KwK 40, entered the PzKpfw IV's production line in March 1942. The decision to adopt this new gun for the PzKpfw IV led to cancellation of the Ausf F production but only after issuing 470 instead of the 500 ordered (the number of vehicles produced varies in different sources, though the deviations are only small).

Owing to the situation immediate production of the new long-barrelled version was begun. At the beginning the L/43-armed PzKpfw IVs were designated as Ausf F/2, subsequently all older L/24-armed Ausf F were renamed Ausf F/1. However, soon the name of the new production run became Ausf G. The changeover led to a short loss of production in March 1942, but in April 80 machines were built. The L/43 gun was in production until April of 1943. Initially, a ball-shaped muzzle brake was used, which was soon replaced by a double-baffle muzzle brake.

Both Ausf F/2 and G were more or less identical to the Ausf F. The only changes introduced were linked to the new ordnance. The troops handled the situation pragmatically; the L/43 armed tanks were commonly called PzKpfw IV *langrohr* (l – long); the older PzKpfw IV *kurzrohr* (k – short).

On 4 April Hitler requested a demonstration of new weapons, among them the PzKpfw III with 5cm KwK L/60, the PzKpfw IV with long 7.5cm KwK(l) and the StuG with long 7.5cm KwK(l).

The 7.5cm KwK 40 fired the following ammunition:

7.5cm SprGrPatr 34: This was the standard HE round fitted with impact fuze AZ 23 to be fired with or without delay.

7.5cm PzGrPatr 39: This was the standard APCBC shell to combat tanks.

7.5cm PzGrPatr 40: As with the 3.7cm and 5cm tank and anti-tank guns, a *Sondermunition* (special ammunition) with tungsten core was available for the 7.5cm KwK 40 Hartkern (HVAP – high velocity, armour-piercing). The restricted supply of tungsten led to a very small number being available. PzGr 40 projectiles were to be saved for combating heavy tanks only. Their effective range was lower than that of the PzGrPatr 39.

7.5cm PzGrPatr 40 (W): This round was externally identical to the standard PrGrPatr 40. The tungsten core was however replaced with unhardened steel. According to a document, this round was to be produced only when tungsten was not available for the PzGr 40. Thus the production facilities of the high-performance round could be permanently used. The performances were much inferior to those of the PzGr 39, see chart.

7.5cm GrPatr 38: *Hohlladungs-Geschosse*, shaped-charge projectiles (HEAT) were an effective and cost-effective shot, though accuracy was reduced by the slow muzzle velocity and high trajectory. During the war,

7.5cm KWK 40 L/43

Calibre:	7.5cm
Length of gun barrel:	3,218mm (L/43)
Range (maximum):	8,000m (auxiliary aiming device)
Velocity (GrPatr 34):	550mps
Velocity (GrPatr 38 [HI/B]):	450mps
Velocity (PzGrPatr 39):	770mps
Velocity (PzGrPatr 40):	990mps
Traverse:	360°
Elevation:	-10° to + 20°
Rate of fire:	10 – 20rpm
Weight:	670kg

three versions (HL/A, HL/B and HL/C) were introduced with improving performance.

7.5 cm NbGrPatr: This round was used for smoke firing.

[Note: The German classification system or the naming of weapons was not always clear. The term 'Panzergranatpatrone' (PzGrPatr) was used to describe a projectile, 'patrone' meaning shell or cartridge. In official documents as well as in the troops' own documents, the shorter synonym '*Panzergranate*' (PzGr) was also used.]

The production statistics for 1942 are difficult to interpret – German units were in constant combat on two fronts, resulting in great and steady losses; the actual stocks were continuously subject to change. Furthermore, quantities were reissued following general refurbishment in the factories.

The *Waffenamt* published lists on tank repair issues on a monthly basis. Although interesting, their informative value is limited due to missing extra information. For instance, by 31 October 1942 the total number of PzKpfw IVs waiting to be refurbished 'in the factories' was quoted as 120. During November a further 15 were added. In the same month seven repaired PzKpfw IV were accepted as being intact. The list also quotes accumulated figures from 5 September 1939 to 30 November 1942; this total number of PzKpfw IV being sent to the factories for general overhaul was 526; 338 were repaired during this period, 341 were accepted as being intact by the ordnance office. 49 were scrapped, the rest were still to be repaired.

The total number of these repaired PzKpfw IV is surprisingly large; the whereabouts of these vehicles is, however, unknown. Some will have been sent to training and replacement units, others will have been reissued to frontline units. Nothing is known about subsequent *Formänderungen* (production improvements) added to older versions. This approach would however explain

Far left: The arrival of PzKpfw IV (lang) was welcomed by tank crews in both Russia and North Africa. Note, the thick layer of dust on the 7.5cm ammunition which could possibly cause a misfire in the breech.

PzKpfw IV Ausf G

Weight:	24,000kg
Engine:	Maybach HL120 TRM
Performance:	265hp
Speed (maximum):	40kph
Range on (road):	210km
Range (cross country):	130km
Trench crossing:	2.3m
Fording depth:	80cm
Ground clearance:	40cm

Spring 1943: A PzKpfw IV Ausf G being unloaded from a *Marinefährprahm* (landing barge) in Tunisia.

PzKpfw IV production 1942

	Production	Actual cumulated stocks
January	59	513
February	58	530
March	8	534
April	80	552
May	85	609
June	72	681
July	88	723
August	84	761
September	93	842
October	99	863
November	113	901
December	155	957

photos showing PzKpfw IV Ausf D being rearmed with 7.5cm KwK 40. This rearming was demanded by Hitler during a lecture dated 13 August 1942:

> The Führer emphasized that all requisites have to be provided to install the new long guns to all PzKpfw IV and *Sturmgeschütz* being sent for refurbishment.

Refurbished tanks were generally not welcomed by the troops. Single components such as engines, transmissions or steering brakes were worn out despite being repaired, leading to continual unreliability in the field.

On 17 May 1942 Albert Speer, who had become *Rüstungsminister* (secretary of armaments) in February, informed Hitler about problems regarding the production of tank spare parts. He suggested reducing the monthly output for PzKpfw II and III to increase spare parts output. The Führer agreed on this temporary measure but insisted on production of both long-barrelled PzKpfw IV and *Sturmgeschütz* carrying on, as these were considered war-winning weapons.

This PzKpfw IV Ausf G from PzRgt 8 (15.PzDiv) has lost the turret stowage box in combat. The mud-covered running gear indicates that there has been recent heavy rain in the desert.

Above: A PzKpfw IV from an unknown unit has more than 20 'kill rings' painted on the gun barrel. Fuel supply in Russia was erratic, so the crew has loaded a 200-litre drum containing petrol on the engine cover.

Right: For some inexplicable reason, production PzKpfw IV were not, for a long time, fitted with carriers for spare track links at the factory. These would be fitted on delivery at an HZA or by workshop units.

Above: In 1942, the HWa issued an order for the front armour on all 7.5cm *Langrohr*-armed PzKpfw IV to be increased from 50 to 80mm. But because of weight considerations the armour on the front of the turret could not be improved.

Left: The result of a driver error: a PzKpfw IV Ausf G hangs perilously on the edge of a deep gully.

Reinforcements began to reach the struggling *Afrika Korps* in December 1942. The crew of this PzKpfw IV Ausf G from PzRgt 7 (10.PzDiv) has loaded a large number of Jerrycans, some filled with water, others fuel, after being made aware of the difficult supply situation in the desert.

Organization

Through 1942 the basic organization of the Panzer divisions was untouched. Each PzAbt had a *Stabskompanie* (staff company), two le PzKp (light tank company to KStN 1171) and one m PzKp (medium tank company to KStN 1175). The company's individual tank strength was very different from unit to unit, depending on the absolute number of available tanks, and in particular PzKpfw IV. At the beginning of *Fall Blau*, the advance to the oil field of the Caucasus, the ratio between PzKpfw III and 38(t) and PzKpfw IV remained unchanged.

However, with growing numbers of Langrohr-armed PzKpfw IV, the tank's slow conversion from the support role to the most important German main battle tank took place (the term main battle tank [MBT] emerged during the mid-1960s).

Experience Reports: PzKpfw IV (lang) in the Desert

The first ten Ausf F2 sent to North Africa arrived at PzRgt 8 in May 1942. The vehicles were welcomed, since they provided a degree of superiority on the desert front.

On 11 August 1942, the staff section of the *Deutsches Afrika Korps* reported (the L/43-armed tank was known as PzKpfw IV (*Spezial* – special):

> Tactical experiences and suggestions for improvement regarding the PzKpfw IV with 7.5cm KwK L/43
>
> 1) Thanks to its high penetration force and accuracy the gun proved superior to all hitherto used weapons during the first engagements. The PzGrPatr 39 pierces at 1,500m the frontal armour of all American and English tanks including the 'Pilot' encountered on the North African theatre. At ranges over 1500m accuracy will decrease (flickering impedes clear observation). With a clear view the lighter tank types were destroyed at 2,000m.
>
> 2) Soon the tank was considered extremely dangerous by the enemy, and due to its distinct shape it attracted the concentrated fire of aeroplanes, artillery and anti-tank guns. For this reason, the PzKpfw IVs have to be guarded by 5cm tanks (PzKpfw III). It is advisable to hold back the tank until rewarding targets such as 'Pilot' are encountered. Flank protection is of great importance. A combined deployment of PzKpfw IV lang seems not to be advisable.

When the 7.5cm KwK 40 L/43 entered service, German tank crews were ordered to conceal the new gun by wrapping straw matting around the barrel. A PzKpfw IV Ausf F2 from PzRgt 7 (10. PzDiv) in Tunisia; the crew are wearing the green-coloured uniform and lace-up boots issued for hot or desert conditions.

3) The tank should not be assigned to recce squads or for flank protection. It should be used only in focal points.

4) It is wrong to fire more than only a few rounds from a position. The muzzle flash and great formation of dust will attract combined fire from the enemy artillery.

5) The PzKpfw IV *Spezial* should not be used as a command tank, it should be nevertheless be fitted with both radio receiver and transmitter.

6) As long as these tanks are available in limited numbers it is necessary to supply them with ammunition by armoured vehicles during combat. The divisions consider essential the deployment of small tanks, armoured personnel carriers or other armoured vehicles.

7) Muzzle blast and dust make target observation difficult, especially on sandy ground.

8) So far the long barrel did not prove disadvantageous, even on undulating ground.

9) We would suggest softening the adjustment of the springing to absorb heavy thrusts on rocky ground.

10) The turret and superstructure roof should be reinforced. A bullet deflector should be mounted to protect the commander's cupola.

11) The gun barrel needs a travel lock. This device should be releasable from the inside. The reason for this measure is that violent shocks can damage the barrel's guide rings.

When a German tank became immobilized on the battlefield and recovery was impossible, the crew were ordered to destroy their vehicle. This was usually achieved by igniting fuel which would then cause the ammunition to explode. Here, it appears the crew has used an explosive charge to destroy the barrel and breech mechanism.

12.) A second ventilator should be mounted to extract powder fumes quicker and more efficiently. Reason: The powder gases impede observation through the vision slits. The sharp smell affects the crew considerably. For the same reason a quick removal of spent shell cases is necessary.

Camouflage was important in the wide, open expanse of the Tunisian desert, since aircraft of the Royal Air Force (RAF) patrolled the skies virtually unchallenged.

All these observations correlate with other recorded experiences. The wish to adjust the spring system is interesting; it shows a certain lack of technical understanding. The simple leaf spring system could not be adjusted.

The *Waffenamt*'s liaison officer to *Panzerarmee Africa* submitted a report dated August 1942:

Tanks: Of all our tanks only the new PzKpfw III with 5cm KwK L/60 and the PzKpfw IV with the KwK 40 fully comply with the requirements of the desert war.

Compared with the latest enemy tanks (identical operational strength provided), the PzKpfw III (L/42 and L/60) proved superior to the British Mk II (Matilda II), Mk III (Valentine), Mk IV (Churchill) and Mk VI (Crusader). The PzKpfw IV with 7.5cm KwK 40 is superior to all encountered enemy tanks, including the American Pilot.

According to the troops' opinion the PzKpfw IV with short 7.5cm KwK is not suited for deployment on the African battlefield.

The crew of a PzKpfw IV Ausf G PzRgt 5 go about their daily ablutions under the cover of palm trees at an oasis in the Tunisian desert.

In mid-1942, many of the combat vehicles earmarked for deployment on the treeless steppe of southern Russia were camouflaged with ochre stripes painted over sand yellow.

During the first half-year of 1942 the majority of British tanks were still equipped with QF 2 pounder guns only. This gun proved ineffective against the newer versions of the PzKpfw III and IV with their face-hardened 50mm frontal armour. Furthermore, the lack of high-explosive rounds considerably limited effectiveness.

The name 'Pilot' referred to the American-built M3 medium tank (Lee and Grant). The deployment of this tank to the British troops marked a watershed. Although the tank's design was criticized, the tank brought much-needed firepower to the British forces. Until the M4 Sherman could be delivered, this tank guaranteed a rough stalemate on the desert front. With the M4 Sherman the Americans succeeded in creating a versatile universal tank, which in some respects would become the Western Allies' T-34.

Tank strength: 31 August 1942, *Panzerarmee Afrika*

Type	Number
PzKpfw II	19
PzKpfw III (5cm kurz)	93
PzKpfw III (5cm lang)	73
PzKpfw IV (7.5cm kurz)	10
PzKpfw IV (7.5cm lang)	27
PzBefWg	6

However, *Panzerarmee Afrika* would be equipped only hesitantly and with comparatively few Panzer IV (lang). The reason for this was the fact that German industry could only produce between 70 and 80 vehicles per month in mid-1942. Presumably the threat of British and American tanks in North Africa was not considered to be a decisive factor, as the comparatively high number of available Panzer III lang indicates. The offensive towards the Caucasus was undoubtedly of greater importance to the planners of the *Organisationsabteilung* (OrgAbt – planning and organizations department).

Fall Blau (Plan Blue) – Into the Caucasus

When Hitler gave marching orders for *Fall Blau* (Plan Blue), nine Panzer divisions, five InfDiv (mot) – motorized infantry divisions with a PzBtl each – one SS division and five StuG-Abt were called upon. The advance started at the end of June 1942. This came as a surprise to the Soviets, who had expected a further offensive heading for Moscow.

The available PzKpfw IV *Langrohr* were issued to these units in numbers ranging from four to twelve. Of interest is that five infantry divisions were

The crew of a PzKpfw IV Ausf G, armed with a 7.5cm KwK L/43, in service with PzRgt 5 (15. PzDiv) have established their camp and prepare for a night in the Tunisian desert.

This PzKpfw IV Ausf F was immobilized by a transmission failure. To make the tank moveable, engineers have removed the final-drive units and guided the track over the return rollers.

issued with a PzAbt each, enhancing their combat power markedly. Further PzKpfw IVs were sent as replacement deliveries during the course of the campaign, but exact figures are not available.

On 1 July 1942, 16.PzDiv reported their *Panzerlage* (tank strength):

39 III kurz, 18 III lang, 15 IV kurz and 12 IV lang

Three weeks later, on 21 July a new report was submitted. The striking increase in the number of Panzer III lang cannot be explained:

Tank strength: July 1942, HG Süd, raid to the Caucasus

Type	Number
PzKpfw II	264
PzKpfw 38(t)	114
PzKpfw III (5cm kurz)	357
PzKpfw III (5cm lang)	545
PzKpfw IV (7.5cm kurz)	148
PzKpfw IV (7.5cm lang)	125
PzBefWg	31
StuG	150

17 III kurz, 70 III lang, 7 IV kurz and 15 IV lang

A report submitted by PzRgt 204 (22.PzDiv) by 20 May 1942 recorded how effective the PzKpfw IV lang proved in combat:

Report on tanks with new ordnance:

The successful advance of 22.PzDiv to Arma Eli was significantly influenced by the new weapons.
Issued with 12 PzKpfw IV KwK 40 and 20 PzKpfw III KwK 39 PzRgt 204 destroyed 50 Russian tanks, among them 12 KV and three T-34. KV tanks were successfully engaged at ranges of 1,200m.
The majority of destroyed tanks showed clear penetrations by 7.5cm ammunition. Most penetrations were detected at the turret front and the hull sides. Most vehicles have burnt out.
During combat ejection problems emerged impairing the deployment. Partially the cartridges had to be manually pushed out using the cleaning rod from outside the vehicle. Possible causes have to be examined.

The crew of a Pzkpfw IV Ausf F take a break during a transfer march in Russia. Note the *Maschinengewehr* (MG – machine gun) 34 in the *Fliegerbeschussgerät* (anti-aircraft mounting).

A PzKpfw IV Ausf G has become immobilized after damaging a track when crossing a railway line.

Both PzGrPatr 39 and 40 and the high-explosive shells have fully met expectations. All questioned commanders and crews revealed that each single hit led to the tank's total destruction. The PzGrPatr 40 was used occasionally only, since PzGrPatr 39 proved entirely successful at all combat ranges.

The tanks with new ordnance have proved effective in combat against the heaviest Soviet tanks. All crews have unanimously declared that they now feel superior to all enemy tanks.

On 6 June 1942, 3.PzDiv reported on their experiences while fighting around Kharkov [*Charkov*]:

General combat experience: The Russian infantry is bad. It does not attack without tanks. The way they attack hasn't changed at all. The attack is still carried out in packs. In spite of a repulsed attack, it will be repeated in the same form again and again, without leading to different results. The Russian infantry cannot stand a determined German tank attack.

The Russian tank weapon is good, the level of training is also good. The statements of a First Lieutenant of their tank force captured near Charkov show that the Russians feel superior to the Germans when fighting in tanks. The use of German hollow-charge

ammunition was known to the Russian officer, but the Russians did not know about the *Panzerkampfwagen* IV with long barrel [the tank was not used at Charkov]. The Russian tank man is very sensitive to fire, even from weapons that cannot harm him. Flanking fire from 3.7cm, 5cm PaK or 5cm KwK L/42 will always cause him to turn off. In some cases this was achieved by machine gun fire. In all cases, hardly any damage could be detected on the bombarded tanks. Because of the limited radio equipment and the missing observation possibilities to the side the Russian is unable to lead his tank attacks in thoroughly combined combat. Thus, for instance only four tanks appear at first, which are gradually followed by others: the Russian is a master in recovering tanks.

The Russian knows that German breakthroughs generally occur along major roads. He has therefore succeeded several times in stopping the advance by two or three T-34s which he has placed or even buried at dominant heights. Well camouflaged, these can only be spotted after opening fire. The positions are chosen in a way that the tanks could not be fought successfully even from the flank. The current commander of the 3.PzDiv has achieved great successes by not advancing along the major roads, but by leaving them out at first.

The Russian air force is also good and extremely numerous. It is dashing in action.

The following new weapons have appeared: British Mk II tanks and American M3 tanks. According to statements made by captured Russians, a super-heavy tank is expected

The crew of this PzKpfwIV Ausf G has ignored authority and reinforced armour protection by placing track links on the front areas of their tank.

Grenadiers supported by tanks in textbook fashion: Two Panzer IV Ausf G, with their turrets guarding each side, advance towards a wooded area. The infantry prepare to engage the enemy with fire from a *Maschinengewehr* (machine gun) 34 mounted on a *Lafette* (carriage) 34.

Two PzKpfw IV Ausf G
from 3.PzDiv: Both are
fitted with *Winterketten*
(winter tracks) which
became available in the
winter of 1942.

to be delivered this year. These are to have armour up to 200mm thick and multiple armament. The calibre of the weapons could not be determined. This would also explain the purpose of the new Russian heavy bridge unit known since autumn. These statements are to be understood with reservations.

The 3.PzDiv had only one armoured half-track company. The commander hopes to establish a further company soon when the vehicles currently being in Krakow for overhaul are returned.

Rumours that the quality of Russian tank steel had deteriorated were vigorously denied. However, it has been determined that the penetration rates are better in the warm season than in the cold, which, in the opinion of the HWa office, is due to the temperature differences.

PzRgt 6 proposes to make the turret numbers of the commander and chief tanks more inconspicuous. The regiment has had bad experiences with the previous numbers. Many leaders of the first and second command level have already been shot down, the third level already also shows considerable gaps. The Russian shows great skill in identifying and shooting out these tanks. At the moment especially the *Panzerbefehlswagen*, which can be recognized by the large and conspicuous frame antennas, are targets of his combined fire.

We recommend that the companies be supplied with interpreters as far as possible. The interpreter can ride along sitting on the gearbox, making it possible to ask locals for direction during the march or attack.

In the fight against enemy tanks it has been shown that calm waiting is often better than dashing attack. Thus, high kill scores can be achieved with low losses. The value of this tactic becomes apparent when comparing the success of 3.PzDiv with that of 23.PzDiv. Slow and gradual approach to the front and flank, then massive attack by the main force on the flanks is appropriate. Tank positions, especially for the precious Panzer IV *Langrohr*, which are still available in small numbers only, must be explored on foot. The tanks must then also be instructed on foot. If the first three shots are not successful, for whatever reason, a change of position must be made immediately.

A PzKpfw IV Ausf G fitted with *Winterketten* is followed by a Krupp Kfz 69 Protze of the divisional PzJgAbt. Note the vehicle is carrying a 3.7cm *Panzerabwehrkanone* (PaK – anti-tank gun).

This statement is full of interesting information. Again, prisoners of war announced the imminent presence of utopian heavy tanks. The writer of the report then tries to reinforce this legend with a Russian heavy-duty bridge.

The adaptation of their own tactics to changed Russian tactics is a sign of the flexibility and acuity of German leadership at battlefield level. Conversely, the Russians often proved incapable of reacting intelligently to such changes.

Right: To enable engine starting in the extreme cold of a Russian winter, a heated water transfer unit was introduced for all tank units.

Below: It was also standard practice to use a specially adapted pressure blowlamp to heat the lubricant in the inertia starter which had solidified due to the cold.

On 7 May 1942, Speer informed Hitler about plans to increase the armour of the *Sturmgeschütz* to 80mm. Necessary work was to be immediately undertaken. Parallel to this a further increase of armour protection for the PzKpfw IV was discussed. Only shortly before, with the beginning of production of Ausf F, the armour of the front of the hull and turret had been increased to 50mm. It was clear that any one-sided increase of armour would be made at the expense of mobility and would result in a shift of the centre of gravity.

The production histories of PzKpfw IV and *Sturmgeschütz* had run in tandem from the beginning, despite their conceptual differences and the fact that different chassis were used. Both shared the same gun and the same roles as 'support vehicles'. Interfering in complex technical questions, Hitler demanded during a *Führerbesprechung* (lecture to the Führer) dated 4 June 1942 that the armour of both StuG and PzKpfw IV should be increased to 80mm as soon as possible. He considered the proposed date of mid-July as being too late.

At this time Hitler's preference for 'heavy' and 'very heavy' tanks emerges. He repeatedly emphasised that a reduced speed caused by an increase of armour could be accepted.

On 29 June, Hitler decreed that the PzKpfw IV was to be fitted with extra armour only to a limited extent; he suggested a monthly share of 16 vehicles (approximately 20 percent of the production). Sometime later, on 14 October

A PzKpfw IV Ausf G from 1.SS-PzDiv Leibstandarte Adolf Hitler (LAH): Note this unit used low-visibility numbers on the turret and also that a non-standard antenna deflector has been mounted on the gun housing.

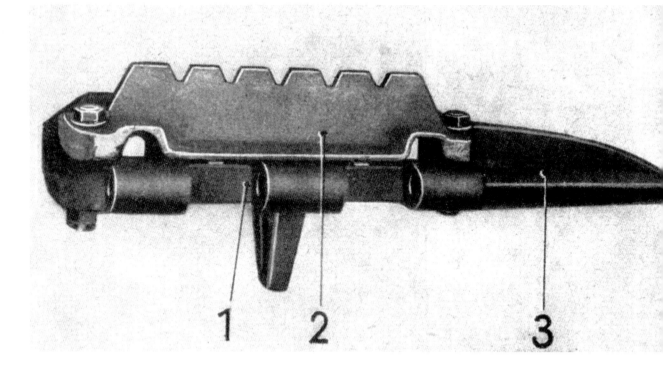

1   **2**   **3**

Above: *Winterketten* (winter tracks): (1) the standard track link; (2) the ice cleat which was bolted on the track link; (3) the extension plate (on Allied tanks these were known as 'Spuds').

Right: PzKpfw IV Ausf G chassis No.82078 (stencilled above the driver's visor) has been fitted with *Winterketten*. Although they improved mobility, the tracks were easily damaged if the suspension was unevenly loaded. The crewmen wear padded winter uniforms and felt boots which became available for winter 1942.

he changed his attitude during another *Führerbesprechung*:

> The Führer considers that facing the steady increase of armour from the enemy tanks, a larger share of the PzKpfw IV must be fitted with *Vorpanzer* (add-on armour).

And by 8 November:

> It is specified that 50 percent of the running production will be provided with *Vorpanzer*. According to many troop reports the *Vorpanzer* of the PzKpfw IV has proven excellent despite the mobility problems involved. Since the British Sechspfünder-PaK [QF 6 Pounder] penetrates the current armour [50mm] of a PzKpfw IV at a distance of 1,000m.

The '*Vorpanzer*' consisted of additional 30mm armour plates. These plates were initially welded to the front of the hull and superstructure. It proved, however, impossible to reinforce the front of the turret.

Later, bolted-on armour plates were also used. There is hardly any system recognizable, every kind of combination was possible. The *Vorpanzer* continued to be added until the use of 80mm armour on the front of the hull and superstructure was implemented as standard in June 1943.

A PzKpfw IV Ausf G in service with 1.SS-PzDiv Leibstandarte Adolf Hitler (LAH). Note the damaged extension plate on the track over the idler wheel. The tank in the background is a PzKpfw III Ausf N armed with a 7.5cm KwK L/24.

PzRgt 33 (9.PzDiv) used small black turret numbers to indentify their tanks. Note the gun is fitted with a single-baffle muzzle brake.

Improving Mobility

The campaign in the east revealed numerous problems. The PzKpfw IV, as with all other German tanks, had been designed for the Central European theatre with its well-developed road network and moderate temperatures. The first campaigns were fought without any problems related to mobility.

The campaign in the East would soon demonstrate the method's limitations. The climate in European Russia is one of hot summers and very cold winters. The country has a great water wealth, its western parts being crossed by hundreds of rivers and streams. The road infrastructure was underdeveloped, relying on the railway.

The weather is treacherous. July is the rainiest month, and despite the often-high temperatures, the sheer amount of water can turn complete areas into swamps. Winter begins in October, and at the turn of the year enormous masses of snow will block any traffic. Temperatures can drop to -40 degrees centigrade and lower. After the winter, snow melt will bring mud, again blocking any movements.

A comparison between the PzKpfw IV and the T-34 is revealing. Like the PzKpfw IV the Soviet medium tank was designed for the climatic conditions in the country of its origin.

The T-34 had wide closed-pattern tracks resulting in a much lower ground pressure compared to the PzKpfw IV. This design prevented the tank from sinking into mud and snow (within specific limitations). The Christie-type running gear consisted of large-diameter disc wheels which prevented mud from entering the suspension.

The suspension system allowed a much faster speed over rough terrain. Compared to the Maybach petrol engine, the diesel engine fitted in the T-34 was far more powerful.

The coming modern German tank developments, the Tiger heavy and the Panther medium tank, were in some respects influenced by the T-34.

However, these tanks were not available in mid-1942. Accordingly, attempts were made to provide the existing tank types with auxiliaries to overcome the mobility problems. The most important German tanks – the PzKpfw III and IV – and the *Sturmgeschütz* used the same tracks, and here the first measures were taken. The tracks were of open-work construction, leading to sinking and allowing mud to pass into the suspension. This problem was accepted since only a fraction of the tank's life was spent in mud or snow, so

The crew of this PzKpfw IV has attached a number of *Stielhandgranate* (stick hand grenade) to the side of the turret, possibly for combat against dug-in infantry or a Red Army anti-tank team.

the loss of efficiency was more than outweighed by the saving of track weight for general service.

For deployment on snowy or icy roads, ice chevrons were available, which could be clipped into the centre of the original 38cm link. With the Ausf F a wider 40cm track was introduced. For this track longer cleats were provided to be attached to the track link's flanks. These performed better on icy roads. However, all these auxiliaries suffered badly from wear and tear. Furthermore, when driving on paved roads the running wheels' rubber bands were heavily affected.

For usage with tracked and half-tracked vehicles small snow ploughs were fabricated. The ploughs did not exceed the width of the tanks' hull and served only to skim/lead away the snow to the tracks where it was compressed, thus clearing a path for following vehicles. These plows were not intended to clear roads of snow.

Before the onset of winter 1942 a specialized track, the *Schnee-Gleiskette* (snow-ice tracks) or *Winterkette* (winter track) was developed. *Rüstungsminister* Speer reported to Hitler on 2 October 1942 (again it is interesting to note that the Führer was interested in minor problems):

I reported to the Führer that independent from the potential widening of the *Sturmgeschütz* tracks by introducing an interleaved suspension substantial numbers of all *Sturmgeschütz*, PzKpfw III and PzKpfw IV being now available at the front will be issued with winter tracks before beginning of winter. According to the planning 75 percent will be equipped by 1 January 1943. The Führer attached great importance to issuing them for all vehicles in *Heeresgruppe Nord* and *Mitte*.

The track links were similar to the standard 40cm track, but had extensions (Allied forces called them 'Spuds') on their outer sides reaching a width of 55cm, resulting in two laterally reversed types of links. The ground pressure could be reduced by at least 30 percent. In terms of performance the PzKpfw IV ground pressure was almost the same as the T-34.

However, experiences showed that the *Winterketten* extensions tended to frequently break off. Finally, the wider tracks imposed one-sided loads to the running wheels, ruining the rubber-tyred running wheels.

The first PzKpfw IV Ausf H, armed with a 7.5cm KwK L/48 gun, were delivered to front-line units in June 1943. A number of these were then deployed for *Unternehmen Zitadelle* (Operation Citadel); the attack on Kursk which was initiated on 5 July and ended on 12 July 1943.

The year 1943 should have been decisive; great parts of the German army had been defeated at Stalingrad in southern Russia and Tunisia in North Africa, slowly changing the strategic framework.

This had dramatic consequences. In the Mediterranean, as the Western Allies could attack and invade Sicily, with the next target being Italy. The Soviet Union quickly recaptured the huge territory gained by the Germans in late 1942. After the catastrophe of Stalingrad in early 1943 the entire southern German Eastern Front was threatened with collapse. In the course of the Voronezh-Kharkov operation, the Red Army was able to retake the city of Kharkov (Charkow) in February 1943. Erich von Manstein, however, succeeded in stabilizing the southern flank and recapturing the city with a brilliant strategic manoeuvre. As a result, Belgorod was also retaken on 18 March.

During this fighting, the number of PzKpfw IVs had risen considerably. The units involved were mainly SS Das Reich, SS Totenkopf, SS Leibstandarte Adolf Hitler, and also 17. and 23.PzDiv and PzGrenDiv Großdeutschland. The combined strength reports from the end of February show 176 PzKpfw IV lang and 172 PzKpfw III lang (including tanks under repair). The only available PzKpfw VI Tiger Ausf E unit was the s PzAbtz 503 with four operational tanks (plus 14 in the workshop). GD also had a company with an unknown number of Tigers.

The assault against Kharkov was a stunning success against an enemy far superior in terms of personnel and material.

The long-barrelled versions of the PzKpfw III and PzKpfw IV would prove themselves brilliantly. Regardless of these successes, and despite the prospect of soon getting a new main battle tank in the PzKpfw V Panther, two simple facts had to be accepted:

A PzKpfw IV Ausf H of 7.Kp part of PzRgt Hermann Göring was deployed in Italy. The tank turret is fitted with the effective side skirts. The hull lacks all fittings, possibly due to the fragmented landscape of the country.

The commander of a PzKpfw IV Ausf G, camouflaged with whitewash, from 1.SS-PzDiv Leibstandarte Adolf Hitler openly observes the effect of his gunfire, but also presents himself as a target for an enemy sniper.

The German tank force could not do without the PzKpfw III in early to mid-1943

In the long run, the German tank force could not do without the PzKpfw IV lang.

On 23 April 1943 an accumulated strength report of all theatres of war was published by the quartermaster general, giving the following figures:

Total tank stock on all fronts 23 April 1943

Type	Number
PzKpfw III (kurz)	345
PzKpfw III (7.5cm)	146
PzKpfw III (lang)	719
PzKpfw IV (kurz)	107
PzKpfw IV (lang)	521
Tiger Ausf E	70
Command tanks	139

Experience Reports

In March 1943 *Generaloberst* Ebehard von Mackensen, Commander-in-Chief of 1.*Panzerarmee* submitted a very positive report to his tank divisions:

> While being attached to 1.*Panzerarmee*, 11.PzDiv had comparatively high tank kills, which suggested to me that the division used tactics being not generally known. Therefore, I requested the divisional commander *Generalleutnant* Balck, to submit a report. Even though it does not contain any secret means, it is nevertheless important. Balck has added some notes:

> 1. Decisive for the success were well-trained long-serving tank crews having used their combat experience as well as their self-confidence gained through earlier successes. When personnel replacements reach the units, these young crews must first be trained. It is better to deploy fewer tanks than use young crews who have not yet had any front-line experience.
> 2. Any identified enemy should be given the opportunity to get nearer to our positions. The one who only attacks fast is at a disadvantage. It is wise to attack the opponent from a hidden position, if possible, by encountering him from the flanks. In addition, it is often advisable to get ready early in the morning to surprise the enemy.

Two PzKpfw IV Ausf G in service with 2.SS-PzDiv Das Reich. Both tanks are fitted with *Winterketten* improving the mobility in mud and snow, but not so effective on sheet ice.

3. It is necessary to approach with cunning and skill (this is especially true when encountering tanks in villages). Before starting an attack disembarked tankers must identify those enemy tanks that are particularly easy to engage: this 'singular combat' must be thoroughly prepared. Tank vs tank battles in a village should be done step by step, always under mutual cover. These will often last for one hour and longer, depending on the enemy.

4. Signed E von .Mackensen

Winter 1943: Two PzKpfw IV Ausf H follow a PzKpfw V Panther of 2.SS-PzDiv Das Reich along a snow-covered forest track. In the same year, it became standard practice to coat all tanks with *Zimmerit*, an anti-magnetic paste manufactured by Chemische Werke Zimmer AG of Berlin.

The report from *Generalleutnant* Hermann Balck followed:

Experience in the fight against tanks: The division shot 1,000 tanks in the period from 28 June 1942 to 11 March 1943, of which the tank regiment destroyed 664, the other weapons 336, of which 65 were killed by close-combat tank destroyer squads. This compares to a total loss of 50 of our own tanks.

(Regarding the figures, the division notes that, apart from minor discrepancies, it considers them to be correct, since these figures were checked as often and as accurately as possible. Damaged tanks which were blown up as a precaution by the *Pioniere* always confirmed these numbers.)

The number of 'kills' achieved by 11.PzDiv seems hard to believe to an unbiased observer: the ratio between Russian and German losses claimed is 20:1. The commander tried to dispel any doubt in his report by referring to multiple counts. Though the Russian army did have a difficult position as an attacker against a determined and well-trained opponent. The general tactical superiority of the Germans, the better coordinated communication and the partly superior weapon technology made such successes seemingly possible under certain circumstances. In combat against Russian tanks, the tactical capabilities of the German tank units were often to prove decisive, even in the case of technical inferiority and significantly smaller forces. Nevertheless, the enormous numerical and material Russian superiority must not be forgotten.

Over this nine-month period the number of PzKpfw III and IV lang would increase. During the recapture of Kharkov, the PzKpfw IV lang became numerically predominant.

The report written by Balck continues:

> These successes are mainly due to the high morale of the troops, their hard-fighting spirit and the quality of their commanders. Looking back on what has contributed to these successes, there are three main points:
> 1. The division must understand how to force the enemy tank unit to fight under (for him) unfavourable conditions.
> 2. All weapons and all means are to be deployed in the fight against tanks.
> 3. The quality of our tactics.

A PzKpfw IV Ausf G of 2.SS-PzDiv Das Reich tows an Opel *Blitz* (lightning) four-wheel-drive truck fitted with a *Kofferbau* (box body) through the snow. The vehicle is marked with 'FK' which suggest that it is part of a *Feldküche* (FK – field kitchen) unit.

Above: Elements of 1.SS-PzDiv Leibstandarte Adolf Hitler progress along a slush-covered road through a Russian village. The leading tank is a PzKpfw III Ausf M, followed by a column of PzKpfw IV mounting the long-barrelled 7.5cm KwK L/43.

Right: A PzKpfw IV Ausf F mounting a 7.5cm KwK L/43, identified by a single-baffle muzzle brake, passes through a burning Russian village. The tank has been fitted with *Winterketten* (winter tracks).and extended winter tracks.

Balck reports an interesting incident:

> If the moment of surprise of an enemy in position cannot be created by an unexpected advance, it must be forced by tactical means. On 24 January 1943 the division attacked the 5km-long village of Eshnychskaya. In front of the village were 3km of uncovered plain. The village was held by an armoured unit, which was driving back and forth on the village road… preventing any break-in.
> An order was issued for the next day:
> Mock attack on the northern part of the village. Heavy smoke has to be fired. Own troops: Armoured cars and PzKpfw II. Purpose: The Russian tanks must be drawn to the northern part of the village, and then our tanks must break-in in the south supported by artillery and Stuka attacking the enemy tanks in the northern part of the village from behind.
> The plan succeeded completely. After our mock attack, almost all Russian tanks were massed in the northern part. Our own tank attack (six Panzer IV lang) to the back of the enemy was successful, 21 tanks were destroyed at the total loss of one tank. The entire Russian tank company was destroyed.

This success is undoubtedly the result of the correct assessment of an exceptional situation, and can hardly be generalized. However, the PzKpfw IV increased in combat value after the installation of the long-barrelled guns

A PzKpfw IV Ausf H mounting a 7.5cm KwK L/48 (note the double-baffle muzzle brake) in the delivery yard at Nibelungenwerke, St Valentin, Austria. The vehicle is fitted with spatial armour to protect the turret and *Panzerschürzen* (tank skirts) and has been camouflaged by applying *Dunkelgrün* (dark green) patches over *Dunkelgelb* (dark yellow) ground.

The 100th PzKpfw IV Ausf H completed at the Nibelungenwerke factory decorated with propaganda slogans. Note the black canisters, which contained spare *Feltzbalg-Filter* (felt filters), mounted on the side of the superstructure. The tank appears to be coated in red oxide anti-rust paint prior to being painted.

(7.5cm KwK L/43 or L/48) had a positive effect, despite inferior mobility and armour protection.

Another unit involved in the battle for Kharkov was InfDiv 'Grossdeutschland'. On 28 February 1943, the unit delivered a report detailing its tank strength. The division was considered to be one of the elite units and subsequently was better equipped. It had a battalion equipped with PzKpfw III and PzKpfw IV, a heavy company with PzKpfw VI Tiger and a battalion of *Sturmgeschütz* III.

At the end of March, the division sent a experience report to *Heeresgruppe Süd*:

Strength report InfDiv 'Großdeutschland', 14 February 1943

Type	Quantity	Under repair
PzKpfw III Flamm	26	-
PzKpfw III lang	12	1
PzKpfw IV kurz	2	6
PzKpfw IV lang	61	2
Tiger Ausf E	4	5
Sturmgeschütz lang	19	13
Command tanks	8	1

Experiences in tank combat

On request of the HG Süd concerning the reasons for the success in the fight against tanks during the winter battle of Kharkov InfDiv 'Grossdeutschland' reports:

Score for the period from 7 March to 20 March 1943

    T-34 = 250

    T-60 or T-70 = 16

    KV-1 = 3

The tanks were destroyed by the following weapons:

    PzKpfw IV (lang) = 188

    StuG 7.5cm (lang) = 41

    PzKpfw VI Tiger = 30

    7.5cm PaK (towed) = Four

    7.5cm PaK (self-propelled) = Four

    15cm sIG (direct hit) = One

    Hafthohlladung = One

A deterioration of the Russian armour material was not visible. But the armour steel is darker and rougher worked. The tanks show that they were produced in a short time, because they lack any finishing. The turret of the T-34 is no longer made from one piece, but is assembled from individual parts. The armour of many tanks

A number of PzKpfw IV Ausf G in the final assembly hall at Nibelungenwerke, St Valentin. Some have been painted *Dunkelgelb* (dark yellow), whereas others remain in red oxide primer. In the foreground is a chassis for a Ferdinand (*Elefant*) tank destroyer.

Above: A production PzKpfw IV Ausf H fitted with *Panzerschürzen* (side skirts) and spatial armour plates around the turret. The type now has 80mm frontal armour.

Right: To avoid damage during production, the running gear was fitted with blank tracks.

consisted of a steel plate about 1cm, a filling of 6cm cast iron and other material and again a 1cm steel plate.

The leadership of the enemy tanks is bad throughout, although there is an officer in almost every tank. Training and morale of the Russian tank crews have noticeably decreased. The training is mostly done in tank factories. Accuracy of enemy tank gunners when standing is good. The radio equipment seems to have improved (US-supplied radios). Panic-like phenomena are noticeable with the appearance of our Tigers.

The Russian generally does not manage to push forward massive attacks with many tanks, but often launches repeated attacks with four to nine tanks. Further useless assaults were ordered by radio commands, giving false situation reports in order to raise the own morale.

It is advantageous to force enemy tank to start moving; the Tiger is especially suitable for this. If it succeeds to get him by the flank or rear, he will descend completely into confusion and is no longer able to take ordered countermeasures. Then it is easy to destroy the enemy tanks.

It is desirable to supply every PzAbt 3 to 4 Tiger without Panzer III lang in addition to the closed Tiger-Kp of the PzRgt, since the Tiger is very suitable for breaking through well concealed and fortified anti-tank gun positions. It is also responsible for getting the enemy tanks, which are standing and shooting at long range, rolling.

The Russian tank generally carries 100 rounds of ammunition (75 high-explosive and 25 armour-piercing shells). The ammunition has not deteriorated. The grenades

A smaller exhaust silencer (muffler) was first fitted on the Ausf F. From 1943, the application of *Zimmerit* anti-magnetic paste became standard for all production tanks. But each of the three manufacturers, Krupp-Grusonwerke, VOMAG and Nibelungenwerke, applied the paste in very different ways.

not only penetrate the armour of our tanks, but disintegrate inside, so that usually all five men are badly wounded.

Our own *Kopfgranaten* [PzGrPatr 39] are of outstanding effectiveness and have a particularly amazing accuracy. In contrast to this is the PzGrPatr 38 HL/B, which is to be used at a maximum of 500m because of its large dispersion. If the HL/B hits at longest distance, its effect is good. However, the troops have no confidence in the HL/B shell. The increased supply of PzGrPatr 39 is desired.

The *Generalinspekteur der Panzertruppen* (Inspector General of Panzertruppen) commented on the report:

27 April 1943
Subject: Experience report InfDiv 'Grossdeutschland'

The following comments are made on the proposal concerning the use of Tigers: The addition of 3–4 Tigers to each battalion is firmly rejected. The Tiger is a focal point weapon within the tank force. The distribution to two PzAbt is a dispersal of the valuable equipment. The technical supervision – which must be guaranteed especially with the Tiger – is not given with a normal PzAbt. The repair service would have to be completely reorganized.

A PzKpfw IV Ausf H of PzAbt '*Rhodos*'; the battalion was established to defend the Greek island of Rhodes. The turret number '200' indicates that it is the tank used by the commander of 2.*Kompanie* (Kp – company).

His brief verdict is not surprising. The Tigers of the heavy tank divisions were intended for use at focal points only. A dispersion of the valuable vehicles was out of the question. It seems therefore obvious that Guderian's department could not approve the allocation of an isolated s PzKp (Tiger) to a division like GD (normally the s PzAbt had three companies of 14 Tigers each, which could fall back on recovery and repair services of a well-equipped workshop company). It is not known whether GD was comparably as well-equipped with support units.

The trend towards 'pure' equipment of the tank divisions with PzKpfw IV is clear. By far the largest part of the tank kills was achieved by PzKpfw IV lang.

Technical Progress

In May 1943, the next production batch of the BW was initiated; the award of the contract dated back to mid-1942. At that time the PzKpfw IV's basic concept was fundamentally questioned, and by December 1942 a far-reaching change was discussed. Certainly influenced by the T-34's design,

The idler wheel is missing on this PzKpfw IV Ausf H: Note that the large number of empty ammunition cases suggest that the tank is being used to attack a distant target prior to an assault by armour and infantry.

German engineers use a Bilstein petrol-electric powered turntable crane to lift a replacement Maybach HL 120 TRM engine into a PzKpfw IV Ausf F.

the coming 9./BW, or Ausf H, should have had sloped frontal and side armour, both having 50mm thickness. Roof and bottom armour were to be reinforced, and the turret was to be simplified. The overall weight was expected to reach 28,450kg. To compensate, it was planned to introduce a widened track supported by triple running wheels.

All these modifications were quickly considered to overburden the basic PzKpfw IV's design, which had already reached a weight of 25,401kg with the up-armoured Ausf G, a gain of some 7,100kg when compared to the Ausf A of 1938.

During a presentation to the Führer on 6 March 1943, Speer noted:

> I have reported to the Führer that with respect to the recently decided further increase of PzKpfw IV production, and referring to the additional weight of the *Schürzen* the *Panzerkommission* had decided to cancel the transition to sloped frontal armour.

The Ausf H entered production without any significant improvements. The essential detail changes were:

Introduction of 80mm armour on both the hull and superstructure front. Besides improving the protection this measure simplified production. This measure was implemented during production; a number of tanks were delivered with 50mm plus 30mm front armour.

The turret's roof plate was reinforced.

The final drive was reinforced. A higher gear ratio reduced the top speed to 38kph.

PzKpfw IV Ausf H

Weight:	25,400kg
Engine:	Maybach HL120 TRM
Performance:	265hp
Speed (maximum):	38kph
Range (road):	210km
Range (cross country):	130km
Trench crossing:	2.3m
Fording depth:	80cm
Ground clearance:	40cm

Panzerschürzen

Prior to the war anti-tank rifles were in the arsenal of almost all nations' armies. These 'heavy rifles' were cheap, easy to operate and effective against contemporary tanks with relatively light armour. With the increase of armour thickness the importance of anti-tank rifles decreased.

However, the Soviet-built 14.5mm *Protivo Tankovoya Ruzhye Degtyaryova* (PTRD – Degtyaryov single-shot anti-tank weapon) 41 and semi-automatic PTRS (S – Simonov) 41 were exceptions. Their calibre was very big, 14.5mm, and accordingly the standard bullet could penetrate 25mm at 100m, the tungsten core ammunition as much as 40mm. These statistics were of course influenced by many external factors. The relatively low costs of this weapon and the unlimited human resources of the Red Army would lead to production of very great numbers. The total output might have exceeded 500,000 rifles. Whole battalions were in action, equipped only with anti-tank rifles.

Both *Sturmgeschütz* and Panzer crews were deeply worried about these weapons. Enemy anti-tank teams could easily hide and wait for the German tanks' approach. At close ranges the side armour of PzKpfw III, PzKpfw IV and StuG could be penetrated under favourable conditions. Vision slits, running wheels and other suspension components could be damaged, and even the commander's cupola was occasionally pierced to lethal effect. Since the anti-tank rifles were not particularly conspicuous either by muzzle flash or smoke, the gunners often remained undiscovered for a long period.

Initially, *Panzerschürzen* were fabricated from mild steel and then armour plate. To save production time and valuable materials, a wire mesh type was introduced for tanks (here a PzKpfw IV Ausf J) on the Russian Front in 1944.

Above: A Red Army infantryman inspects a PzKpfw IV Ausf H which has been knocked out by three hits that have penetrated the *Panzerschürzen* and the 30mm armour of the superstructure.

Right: A PzKpfw IV Ausf H loaded on a railway wagon for delivery to front-line unit. The *Panzerschürzen* and the mounting brackets have been stowed under the hull. Note, the new type of *Fliegerbeschussgerät* anti-aircaft mounting) fitted on the commander's cupola.

In April 1942, PzRgt 6 submitted an after-action report:

> Damage by fire from anti-tank rifles: Direct hits by anti-tank rifles on the reinforced frontal plates resulted in a penetration depth of 25mm. The frontal armour was never pierced. Direct hits to the sides of PzKpfw III and IV did not lead to penetration in most cases. In one case the 30mm side of the turret of a PzKpfw IV was penetrated, but the firing range is unknown.

By early 1943 the first trials with side skirts had been carried out, which turned out to be positive. Although the 14.5mm bullets pierced the 5mm steel plates, the impact was significantly reduced. The impact of 75mm high-explosive shells was also reduced. The plates were heavily damaged or torn off, but the mounting brackets remained intact and the basic armour was not harmed. The tank remained operational.

On 6 March during a lecture to the Führer, *Rüstungsminister* Speer noted:

> I reported to the Führer about the successful firing experiments with *Schürzen*. All *Sturmgeschütz*, Panzer IV and Panthers currently in production must be instantly issued with *Schürzen*. Furthermore, all other vehicles of this type being in combat in the field must be provided with *Schürzen* as quickly as possible. The time schedule for the full conversion has to be submitted quickly.

Reports and orders show that before the attack on Kursk (*Unternehmen Zitadelle* [Operation Citadel]) *Panzerschürzen* for PzKpfw IV, assault guns and PzKpfw III, which were already with front units, were delivered by train to the east. These were assembled by the workshop companies. The conversion was carried out according to the specifications of the local commanders and independent of the equipment status of the vehicles. Even older PzKpfw IV variants, short and long barrelled, were also equipped with *Panzerschürzen*.

Zimmerit

In September 1943 application of an antimagnetic mine coating (*Zimmerit*) was ordered for all tanks and *Sturmgeschütz*. This measure was subsequently introduced to the PzKpfw IV assembly lines.

Although the author could find no document explicitly explaining the reasons for this measure, it seems to be closely linked to the introduction of the German *Hafthohlladung* 3kg by the end of 1942. This magnetic anti-tank weapon had a strong shaped charge (Hl) making it a simple and effective hand-held weapon. Already by January 1943 the HWa had ordered respective trials of counter measures for their own tanks. Several materials were tested:

– thick layers of frozen water
– thick layers of paint
– oily materials (bitumen or tar)
– bitumen and tar mixed with grit
– a thin concrete mix, with or without grit

The ground clearance on this PzKpfw IV Ausf H has been increased by fitting a 10cm spacer under each bogey carrier to create what was known as a '*gestelztes Fahrwerk*' (stilted [raised] chassis). The gas cylinder mounted on the rear indicates that it is in service with an *Ersatz-und-Ausbildungs Abteilung* (Ers u AusbAbt - training and replacement battalion).

Only the thin concrete mix proved to be suited to countering the magnetic adhesion. Work on this concrete-emulsion mixture was forwarded by a firm called Zimmer, hence the name.

After the fluid paste was applied to the tank, a certain pattern was stamped or scratched before curing. These vertical grooves resulted in a scruffy, uneven surface, avoiding greater plate areas spalling off due to machine gun fire or artillery splinters.

It is questionable whether these efforts expended on the tanks were justified. To the author's knowledge the Allies did not use magnetic charges on a large scale, other than when captured German materials were used.

Left: A US Army officer demonstrates the impact of a Bazooka rocket projectile on the wire mesh type of *Panzerschürzen*.

Below: PzKpfw IV Ausf H: note an *Maschinengewehr* (MG – machine gun) 34 has been fitted in the *Fliegerbeschussgerät* (anti-aircraft mounting) attached to the front of the commander's cupola.

A PzKpfw IV Ausf J in service with 18.ArtDiv which was an experimental artillery unit. Note the tank is fitted with wider *Ostketten* (East tracks) for winter conditions.

Attempts to Improve Mobility

As we have noted, the PzKpfw IV was conceived before the outbreak of World War II, so its tactical and technical capabilities were naturally based on the limited experience of the pre-war period and the technical and economic possibilities. The tank was developed for use in Central Europe, taking into account the climatic conditions there.

The unexpected problems during the invasion of Russia quickly showed the limitations of the PzKw IV's design (and of all other German tanks). In this context, the development and introduction of the widened *Winterkette* in 1942 was an economical and, to a certain extent, effective measure to improve mobility in mud and snow.

German reports often complained about the ground clearance of the PzKpfw IV being too low. According to existing original German documents this was 40cm, in contrast the Russian T-34, which had (according to German documents WaPrüf 6) 38cm. Due to the sloped shape of the hull (as well as the wider chains and the much better power-to-weight ratio) its mobility in mud and snow was much better. The PzKpfw IV was handicapped because of its almost vertical front.

In the summer of 1943, a remedy was found in the Nibelungenwerk. The simple design of the suspension allowed a direct intervention. The bogies (four per side), which were attached directly to the hull, were each fitted with

Left: A tank crew crank-up the inertia starter for the Maybach HL 120 TRM.

Below: This photograph (also see page 228) proves that a number, which remains unknown, of *gesteiztes Fahrwerk* fitted PzKpfw IV were used in combat.

two spacers using the existing drill holes. Due to this very simple solution the ground clearance could be increased by about 10cm. The engineers at the Nibelungenwerk proudly pointed out the fact that a number of screws could be saved per tank.

Unfortunately, it is not clear from the accessible documents whether and in what framework this change was introduced. The simplicity of this solution would have allowed retrofitting near the front by the workshop companies.

A document of the *Organisationsabteilung* (OrgAbt – organization battalion) in the *Generalstab des Heeres* (GenStbdH – general staff of the army) from September 1943 proves that the components were in principle available:

Subject: PzKpfw IV with *gestelztem Laufwerk* [stilted (raised) chassis]

Reference: *Chef Heeresrüstung and Befelshaber des Ersatzheered* [GenStbdH – chief army armaments and commander of the replacement army]

GenStbdH requests:

– Immediate production of spacers for increasing the ground clearance for 1,500 PzKpfw IV to be installed by the troop workshops.
– Equipment of all PzKpfw IV from the running production with raised chassis.

This request indicates a troop trial, which has apparently been successful. Nothing is known about the further development. However, photos are known proving the use of the 'stilts' at the front. A general introduction was not made for unknown reasons.

Organizational Changes

Prior to the Kursk campaign the majority of seven Panzer divisions listed only one battalion per regiment, five were still issued with two battalions. This is only a rough guide, since the involved units showed a mixed and inconsistent picture. Most tank regiments and battalions were still furnished with le and m PzKp (light and medium tank companies). The PzKpfw IV were officially issued to the m PzKp, but the unit commanders distributed the tanks over the entire regiment according to the situation.

With the knowledge that the PzKpfw IV was to remain the Panzer division's main weapon in the middle-term, the number of PzKpfw IV per company was constantly increased. By November 1942 a revised organizational structure for the PzKpfw IV was published (KStN 1175, 1 November 1942), authorizing again 14 PzKpfw IV per m PzKp. Finally, by January 1942, a totally new

In July 1943, 1.PzDiv was transferred to Greece. Here a PzKpfw IV Ausf G is seen during a parade in Athens, before the unit was deployed as part of the force sent to defend the south of the country.

structure was issued, authorizing 22 PzKpfw IV per company. The reason for this considerable reinforcement was the wish to standardise the vehicle stock. The increase of PzKpfw IV production made this possible. This new structure was implemented by and by.

In June 1943, the *Oberkommando des Heeres* ordered:

> Reorganization of the Panzer regiments and battalions in the *Ostheer* (East armies).

> By December 1943 it will be definitely be possible to fill up the PzDiv in the East (with one battalion) having 96 PzKpfw each (the majority being PzKpfw IV, with some PzKpfw III lang). Parallel to that it is planned to establish a Panther-equipped battalion for the bulk of the Panzer divisions in the Reich.

Each of the relevant PzAbt was to be reorganized with a staff company, a *Panzer-Flammzug* (flame-thrower platoon) to be established according special order only, four tank companies, and a workshop company.

With the beginning of the assault on the Kursk salient considerable numbers of PzKpfw III kurz (5cm KwK L/42) and PzKpfw IV (7.5cm KwK L/24) were available. The PzKpfw IV lang was the most numerous. The new PzKpfw V Panther tank made its debut, and the PzKpfw VI Tiger Ausf E was aready available in significant numbers.

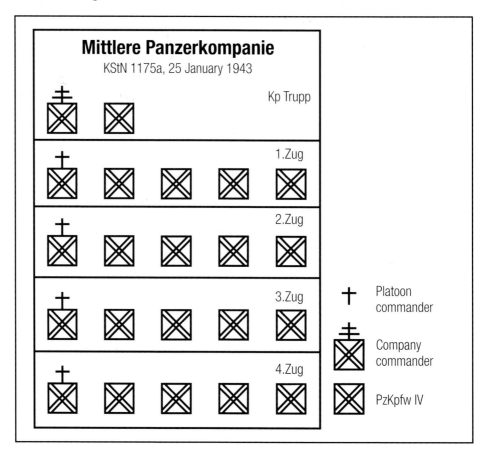

Kursk

The German general staff worked out plans to regain control of operations in the east. Around the city of Kursk a large frontal salient had been established. This salient should be pinched off, considerably shortening the front. In the course of this operation (Citadel) considerable parts of the Russian land forces were to be destroyed, and an important city taken.

After a successful end to the operation, Guderian as the Inspector General of the Armoured Forces hoped that he would have time to finally establish operational reserves for the army.

The Germans mobilized all available forces. 16 Panzer divisions, two PzGrn divisions and four SS divisions were deployed. Additionally, another three Tiger battalions were called in at army troop level. PzRgt 39 was also

to be provided with over 200 Panthers, the first mission for the new main battle tank.

Due to several time delays on the German side, the Russians were warned and in advance, deeply staggered defence positions were established.

The battles around the city were fierce. Tank vs tank engagements took place at very near distances. Tanks like the Tiger Ausf E and the new Ferdinand tank destroyer proved to be relatively immune to gun fire. The Panther medium tank, which, due to its remarkably good characteristics was actually the 'darling' of the German tankers, failed all along the line due to teething troubles during its first deployment. These problems had an almost classic cause: mass production was done without thorough practical testing. Overcoming the teething troubles led to a waste of valuable time.

The PzKpfw IV and III had to attack the enemy positions with great caution, as the danger of running into mines or being shot down by PaK or tanks was too great. Preparatory artillery fire and air raids (the Luftwaffe held a fragile superiority in Russia) were necessary. Technically outdated tanks like the PzKpfw III, no matter if short- or long-barrelled, could be used successfully at the shortest fighting distances (under 50m). The same applied to the Russian T-26 armed with a 45mm cannon. In individual cases surprising successes could be achieved even against Panther and Tiger.

This PzKpfw IV Ausf G was one of those delivered with factory-fitted *Panzerschürzen*; the plates were hung on brackets, fitted with small hooks, and were easily torn off during operations. The tank also has 30mm additional armour welded to the bow and superstructure.

According to an OrgAbt file, the German tank losses during the battle of Kursk were surprisingly low, but Russian losses were several times higher. Nevertheless, the battle had to be stopped – the Russian units were able to fill the gaps and counterattack.

After-action Reports

A look at the PzKpfw IV stocks in a panzer division is interesting. PzRgt 18 (18.PzDiv) reported the following strengths before the attack on Kursk on July 1, 1943: 29 PzKpfw IV lang and five PzKpfw IV kurz, plus 20 Pzkpfw III (7.5cm) and ten Pzkpfw III short.

On 26 August 1943, losses were reported; twelve PzKpfw IV were recorded as total losses:

Date	Type	Chassis No:	Cause
07 Jul	PzKpfw IV L/48	84932	Mine*
08 Jul	PzKpfw IV L/43	82846	Mine*
08 Jul	PzKpfw IV L/48	84914	Mine
09 Jul	PzKpfw IV L/43	83781	Hit by armour-piercing fire from an anti-tank gun and burnt out
09 Jul	PzKpfw IV L/48	83845	As above
14 Jul	PzKpfw IV L/48	83789	As above
16 Jul	PzKpfw IV L/24	82078	Hit by armour-piercing shell*
16 Jul	PzKpfw IV L/24	80859	Mechanical failure*
16 Jul	PzKpfw IV L/24	80978	Mechanical failure*
16 Jul	PzKpfw IV L/48	84090	Destroyed by crew
16 Jul	PzKpfw IV L/48	84259	Demolished
16 Jul	PzKpfw IV L/48	83873	As above

[* Returned by rail to ordnance depot in Magdeburg for major repairs and rebuilding.]

These figures show that the losses were due to very different causes. First of all it is noticeable that only the older variants armed with the 7.5cm KwK L/24 (one Ausf E, one Ausf F) failed due to technical faults. Presumably, the final drives or the steering gears were the cause of the failure here, being more susceptible owing to their age. Although they could be recovered, repair in the field was not possible.

All other vehicles had been destroyed by mines or armour-piercing projectiles. At least half of the total failures were sent to Magdeburg for a general overhaul after recovery.

Probably due to the strained production situation, the responsible persons forced the transport of heavily damaged tanks to companies in the Reich, where

Tank strength as of 1 July 1943, *Unternehmen Zitadelle*

Type	Number
PzKpfw II	107
PzKpfw 38(t)	12
PzKpfw III (5cm kurz)	149
PzKpfw III (5cm lang)	513
PzKpfw III (7.5cm kurz)	191
PzKpfw IV (7.5cm kurz)	54
PzKpfw IV (7.5cm lang)	859
PzKpfw V Panther	200
PzKpfw IV Tiger	147
s StuG Ferdinand	90
StuG	≈ 450
PzBefWg	119

they were repaired. A *Waffenamt* file from October 1942 shows that since September 1939 a total of 499 PzKpfw IV were delivered for general overhaul. Of these, 323 vehicles were completed and 40 scrapped by September 1942.

After the ill-fated *Unternehmen Zitadelle* was cancelled, the Soviets attacked with their reserves at the northern front. The weakened German forces had to retreat. 9.PzDiv and 20.PzDiv were defending this area. As a result, 9.PzDiv created a combat group, *Kampfgruppe* Zimmermann whose commanding officer submitted an after-action report on 29 July.

Tank losses as of July 1943, *Unternehmen Zitadelle*

Type	Number
PzKpfw II	21
PzKpfw 38(t)	3
PzKpfw III (5cm kurz)	18
PzKpfw III (5cm lang)	94
PzKpfw III (7.5cm kurz)	59
PzKpfw IV (7.5cm kurz)	19
PzKpfw IV (7.5cm lang)	252
PzKpfw V Panther	71
PzKpfw IV Tiger	20
s StuG Ferdinand	39
StuG	118
PzBefWg	15

Above: The Kfz 100 was the standard crane truck having a lifting capacity of 3,050kg. The PzKpfw IV Ausf G is in service with 2.PzDiv. The Habsburg '*Doppeladler*' (double-headed eagle) was used by the division since its home garrison was in Vienna and a significant number of crewmen were Austrian.

Right: The chassis of a PzKpfw 38(t), has been converted by field engineers to carry a hand-operated crane.

Combat report for the 28 July 1943

By 02:00hrs the commander at his regimental command post received orders to move to an assembly area near the line Vetrovo–Shamjanskij expecting an enemy assault. By 03:00hrs the tanks moved into an assembly area in a reverse slope position. Three armoured half-track carriers assembled in a depression south of the tanks. On height 233.0 we observed 22 enemy tanks. To provoke an attack we withdrew our left flank in a very conspicuous manner. This feint fully succeeded and the enemy attacked. In a short but fierce firefight 24 enemy tanks, among them three US-built tanks, were destroyed by our Panzer IV lang without a single loss.

At 09:00hrs a most successful StuKa (Ju-87) attack took place; in consequence eight enemy tanks and an assault gun were chased into swampy lowland where they became immobilized. Exploiting the situation, the battle group launched a counterattack. Dismounted riflemen of 20.PzDiv followed the tank assault and cleaned up the battlefield. Despite heavy fire from well-concealed positions the attack quickly gained ground and by noon 2.Kp supported by a tank company took height 233.0; the right flank was protected by 2./PzAbt 21. Now the *Panzergrenadiere* [armoured infantry] of 20.PzDiv occupied positions on height 233.0.

By 13:00hrs the commander reported accomplishment of the mission, by 15:00hrs *Kampfgruppe* Zimmermann was relieved by PzAbt 21 (20.PzDiv).

Above: A recovery team from 20.PzDiv: many Panzer divisions relied on half-tracked tractors to retrieve an immobilized tank. Normally the SdKfz 9 heavy half-track tractor was used, but as here, it was substituted by a lighter SdKfz 8.

Right: In 1943, the Kliment Voroshilov (KV) 85, armed with an 85mm D-5T gun, entered service with the Red Army providing them with a tank which could out-perform a PzKpfw IV Ausf H armed with a 7.5cm KwK L/48.

Below: A PzKpfw IV Ausf H from an unknown unit is fitted the early type *Panzerschürzen* brackets, where each plate carried simple hooks. Note the *Filzbalg-Filter* (felt filters) mounted on the side of the superstructure.

The enemy was apparently shaken and did not attempt a further counterstrike. The *Kampfgruppe* was very successful, destroying 30 tanks, among them six heavy American types. We registered no tank losses. In the course of the assault a further 15 tanks and an assault gun were finished, partly by PzAbt 21 (20.PzDiv); those tanks that got stuck were blown up by our men.

We took 130 prisoners, and captured great amounts of weaponry and equipment. We estimate the enemy lost to 250–300 men. According to interrogations of PoWs the night before three marching battalions had been sent to this sector, which have all been totally battered or annihilated.

On 27 July, one day before this after-action report was written, 9.PzDiv submitted its daily *Panzerlage* (strength report):

Daily report:
Panzerlage (except *Kampfgruppe* Schmahl):
Ready for action: Six PzKpfw III lang; two PzKpfw IV kurz; 29 PzKpfw IV lang and two BefWg.
Short term repair: Nine PzKpfw III lang; Two PzKpfw IV kurz and four PzKpfw IV lang
Long term repair: Five PzKpfw III kurz; three PzKpfw III lang; three PzKpfw IV kurz; five PzKpfw IV lang and one BefWg
Total losses: One PzKpfw IV lang (reason unknown)

An SdKfz 251 with 28-round *Wurfrahmen* (launching frame) for 32cm rockets and a PzKpfw IV have been abandoned, apparently undamaged, by their crews.

Above: The KV-85 utilized a lighter version of the KV-1 chassis which improved mobility. It was fitted with a cast-armour turret which provided good protection and adequate room for three men. It was also the first Soviet tank to have a cupola.

Right: The *Samokhovdnaya Ustanovka* (SU) 152, known as *Zveroboy* (beast slayer), mounted a 152mm ML-20S gun-howitzer which made it the first Russian type capable of defeating a PzKpfw VI Ausf E Tiger.

Above: A further important step taken by Russian military planners to modernize their tank forces was the installation of an 85mm D-5T gun in the T-34. According to German instructional pamphlets, published by the ordnance department, the T-34/85 was far superior to a PzKpfw IV.

Right: Equipment of all types supplied under the Lend/Lease Program was of great importance to the Soviet Union. But the Infantry Tank Mk II Churchill, despite having adequate armour protection, could easily be defeated by a PzKpfw IV armed with a long-barrelled gun.

September 1943: A PzKpfw IV Ausf H from 13.PzDiv on board a *Siebelfähre*, (motor ferry) when the unit was being evacuated from the Kuban bridgehead.

PzKpfw IV production 1943

	Accepted by Waffenamt	Actual cumulated stocks	PzKpfw IV (kurz)	PzKpfw IV (lang)
January	163	1,077	?	?
February	171	1,130	?	?
March	205	975	?	?
April	213	1,018	?	?
May	272	1,077	?	?
June	253	1,211	164	1,047
July	244	1,472	167	1,305
August	283	1,374	158	1,216
September	289	1,360	157	1,203
October	328	1,574	186	1,388
November	238	1,672	184	1,488
December	324	1,951	188	1,763

These numbers show that the long-barrelled PzKpfw IV had become predominant. However, this report gives the number of short-barrelled PzKpfw IV as still seven. The following daily report approves the combat reports submitted by Zimmermann.

In the year 1943 production of the PzKpfw IV was ramped up, pointing to the simple fact that it had become the most important tank in the German arsenal. (From August to October 1943 Bulgaria received a monthly delivery of 15 PzKpfw IV, eight of which were sent to Turkey.) However, it must not be forgotten that parallel to this increase the StuG production reached similar figures, indeed exceeding the PzKpfw IV output by the end of 1943 (3,011 against 2,983). The Panther, being introduced as the PzKpfw IV's successor, reached a production of 1,768 units, an impressive number.

Again, all the 1943 statistics apply to L/24 and L/43 resp L/48 guns. However, for the sake of accuracy the *Rüststand* were broadened from June 1943, now showing separate stocks for *Kurzrohr* (L/24) and *Langrohr* (L/43 also L/48) armed PzKpfw IV. The lists were repeatedly corrected, though the reason is not known. The differences resulting from these corrections are surprisingly high; in August more than 250 vehicles.

The consistent number of short-barrelled PzKpfw IV is revealing. This could indicate that the majority of these vehicles were in the replacement army.

In December 1943, Krupp was ordered to cease production of the PzKpfw IV and instead concentrate on manufacturing the *Sturmgeschütz* IV.

A PzKpfw IV Ausf H in the staff company of I./ PzRgt 1 (1.PzDiv); note an MG 34 has been fitted in the *Fliegerbeschussgerät* (anti-aircraft mounting). The division was deployed in the Balkans from June to September 1943.

July 1943: German tanks advance across the rolling, wide-open steppe of the southern Soviet Union near Belogrod/Orel (Kursk). (Getty)

Italy

After the defeat in Africa, the German High Command expected an Allied landing on Sicily. It finally took place on 10 July 1943 at the same time as the end of the German offensive on the Kursk salient. To cope with this new threat, the 1.SS-PzDiv Leibstandarte Adolf Hitler was transferred from the Eastern Front to Italy in July 1943.

However, this powerful unit (71 PzKpfw V Panther tanks) was to remain in central and northern Italy with one Panzer and one PzGrenDiv and did not enter the battle.

Again the PzKpfw IV was the most numerous tank type, with the *Sturmgeschütz* being second.

On 25 August 1943, the GenInspdPzTrp sent a *Reise-Offizier* (travelling officer) to prepare a report on the deployment of tank units.

A *Zug* (Zg – platoon) of the staff company of I./ PzRgt 1 (1.PzDiv). The staff company was not only tasked with defending the regimental staff: it would also be deployed for reconnaissance duties.

He reported:

Due to the very bad railway connections, the OB *Süd* (Supreme Commander Southern Forces) provided me with a vehicle to visit the individual units. Since these units were spread over a large area in upper, central and southern Italy, I was able to get to know the terrain and the road conditions there quite accurately. A use of tank units seems to be possible only in northern Italy. In central and southern Italy this is only the case in some flatter areas on the east and west coast. The use of tanks in the mountainous parts of Italy [Apennines] is not very promising. The road and terrain conditions are very difficult for transfers from one coast to the other. Although these roads are good throughout and largely dust-free, some of them are narrow and wind up and down in narrow and steep curves. During a land march, materiel is subjected to extremely high stress. Under these conditions and the great heat, the wear of the running wheels especially is very high. The engines overheat very quickly and the support and steering brakes are subjected to extraordinary stress. My impression is that Tiger units are not suited for combat in central and southern Italy. In northern Italy in the river Po plain, the many small canals and irrigation systems are a hindrance. A relatively light, agile and fast tank seems to be best suited for use in Italy.

Despite these clear words, at the turn of the years 1943/44 further units were transferred to Italy, including two s PzAbt with more than 50 Tiger tanks. A further Tiger unit would follow in June 1944.

The required 'light tank' was not available, the new German developments were expected to weigh 50,800kg and more. Reduced to the combat weight, the requirement profile of the 'travel officer' applied only to the PzKpfw IV.

On 19 December 1943, the 6./PzRgt 26 (26.PzDiv) delivered a report of a mission near Orsogna:

On 14 December the company was ordered to advance together with the 1./ InfAbt 9 on the road Orsonga-Ortona to Point 155 in order to seal off the enemy breaking-in there. For this purpose, the combat group (Major Brandt) started at 23:30hrs from Point 280 and reached a group of houses 500m south of Point 155 at 02:15hrs without significant enemy resistance. The point was occupied by a platoon of 1./InfAbt 9 and four PzKpfw IV of the 6.Kp. At 07:20hrs, two enemy tanks, after heavy artillery bombardment, attacked the lead PzKpfw IV coming from the southeast. An enemy Sherman tank received three hits, retreated but became stuck in the water-logged ground after about 1,200m. The second Sherman damaged the PzKpfw IV by two hits on the gun mantlet and the commander's turret and also retreated. All day long heavy enemy artillery fire was laid on Point 155. Our own tanks stayed in position while the infantry retreated about 400m after suffering grievous losses. In the early

Tank strength: 20 August 1943, Italian Front

Type	Number
PzKpfw III (5cm kurz)	2
PzKpfw III (5cm lang)	26
PzKpfw III (7.5cm kurz)	49
PzKpfw IV (7.5cm kurz)	17
PzKpfw IV (7.5cm lang)	318
PzKpfw V Panther	71
StuG	186
PzBefWg	80

morning hours of 16 December, the Brandt group was withdrawn for a new mission, 6.Kp stayed in place alone. Around 05:00hrs the enemy again tried to advance with tanks towards Point 155 after an even heavier artillery bombardment. The attack was repulsed. The area was covered by thick smoke which allowed the enemy tanks to withdraw. A Churchill tank was destroyed by a number of direct hits, and the enemy infantry was repulsed by machine gun fire. We lost a PzKpfw IV to a number of direct hits (one dead, two wounded). Due to the resumption of artillery fire, our tanks were withdrawn by 400m. At 16:00hrs the company was ordered to retreat to Point 181 in the direction of Tollo. The company entered the new area with all tanks still operational without being noticed by the enemy.

Signed *Oberleutnant* Schaft, *Kompanie Führer*

In 1942 large numbers of severely damaged PzKpfw IV Ausf D and Ausf F were returned to Germany to be rebuilt and returned to service. Here a PzKpfw IV Ausf D has been fitted with wider 40cm tracks, an Ausf F drive sprocket, and mounts a 7.5cm KwK L/43. The tank also has a full set of brackets for *Panzerschürzen*.

These lines indicate that in the geographically demanding Italian theatre of war in 1943, the quality of tactical command was of greater importance than the type and extent of armament and armour of the tanks. The PzKpfw IV proved to be absolutely equal to the Sherman and Churchill when used appropriately. Compared to the US-built 75mm M1 or the British 6 Pounder, the German 7.5cm KwK 40 was clearly superior, which compensated for its technical vulnerability.

For all combatants, immediate success depended on other factors. The supply of ammunition and fuel was crucial, as was the degree of artillery or air support.

1944 – Technical Progress 11

With the development and introduction of the modern German PzKpfw V Panther and PzKpfw VI Tiger Ausf E tanks, the German planners intended to achieve a long-lasting superiority on the battlefield. Obviously, all other belligerent nations were anxious to counter this incipient superiority.

While the Western Allies were already advancing in Italy and although a landing on the Atlantic coast was expected at any time, the German General Staff – and especially Guderian – always focused on the situation on the Eastern Front. It seems that in their eyes tank combat in the East was the key. Some officials in the German government dreamed of a separate peace with the Western Allies.

Russia, with its state-controlled, inefficient and technically backward industry (the author is aware of the contradiction in this last description, because both T-34 and KV were the result of innovative engineering work) decided on a consequent technical simplification of these tanks in order to achieve the highest possible output. As Stalin is reputed (wrongly) to have said, 'Quantity has a quality all its own.' For this reason, between 1941 and 1943 few resources were used to develop the tank.

In this context, the enormous human resources of the Soviet Union must not be forgotten, and the unconditional will to use this superiority in military (or human) material ruthlessly. The disproportionate losses of Red Army soldiers are a direct result of this doctrine.

In the course of 1943, the situation was to change slowly. Already during the battle of Kursk an 85mm gun was to be introduced in the heavy KV tank, which would prove its worth in the fight against Panther and Tiger. From summer on, efforts were made to install this gun also in the T-34 mass tank.

The heavy KV tank was now to be further developed. With the Josef Stalin, for the first time a heavy 122mm gun was installed in a tank produced in series with

On 16 December 1944, German forces launched a surprise counterattack which developed into the Battle of the Bulge. The attacking force included 116.PzDiv, whose PzRgt 16 had only 21 PzKpfw IV and 41 PzKpfw V Panther combat ready at that time. The battle ended on 25 January 1945 when German units were forced to retreat.

An abandoned PzKpfw IV Ausf J from 1.SS-PzDiv Leibstandarte Adolf Hitler. The undamaged tank has a complete set of *Panzerschürzen* with improved mounting brackets.

the strongest armour protection. Both tanks were available in 1944 in ever larger numbers.

With their arrival the discontinuation of the PzKpfw IV was again discussed at the end of 1943. Since the assault gun had proved to be a dreaded tank destroyer in the east, an increase in its production was now considered at the expense of the PzKpfw IV. In this situation Guderian, being the creator and apologist of *Panzerwaffe* and in consequence of the PzKpfw IV main battle tank, used all his powers of persuasion to fight for the continuation of PzKpfw IV production.

Before a meeting with the Führer on 5 Sept 1943 he noted the following points:

PzKpfw IV or *Sturmgeschütz?*

Despite reports to the contrary, any superiority of the *Sturmgeschütz* over the PzKpfw IV does not actually exist, because the *Sturmgeschütz*:

–   Has no rotating turret (traverse 24 degrees against 360 degrees) and therefore acts unilaterally forward and has to make time-consuming movements to fire at flank and rear targets.

- Is vulnerable against close-combat attacks (no integrated machine gun) and thus depends on constant protection by attached infantry.
- Has slightly less off-road mobility (it is 1,525kg heavier than a PzKpfw IV).

These tactical and technical disadvantages of the assault gun are not compensated for by its advantages compared to the PzKpfw IV (lower height, frontal armour 80mm against 50mm). The assault gun lacks the decisive, lightning-fast ability to operate in all directions, and the ability to fight without support of infantry if necessary. If the situation requires, the PzKpfw IV can be used in the role of an assault gun.

A conversion of the PzKpfw IV production to assault guns would mean turning a versatile weapon into a one-dimensional weapon. Front reports that speak of the superiority of the *Sturmgeschütz* over the PzKpfw IV are subjective. The assault gun remains with the infantry, the tank will often be withdrawn for other tasks. Therefore, there is great sympathy for the assault gun. Apart from unavoidable delays, the change of manufacture would mean a measure that, once carried out, cannot be undone at will.

Suggestion: No conversion, but deployment of tanks for assault gun missions as far as necessary.

The purpose-built facility known as Nibelungenwerke in *Sankt* (St – saint) Valentin, Austria was the only factory that continued to produce the PzKpfw IV until end of the war – the US Army 259th Infantry Regiment entered St Valentin on 9 May 1945, but on 9 May the Red Army forces occupied the factory. This newly completed PzKpfw IV Ausf J, painted *Dunkelgelb* (dark yellow), is fitted with improved *Panzerschürzen* and brackets. An MG 34 has been fitted in the *Fliegerbeschussgerät* (anti-aircraft mounting).

Crew members of a PzKpfw IV Ausf J, in service with 1.SS-PzDiv Leibstandarte Adolf Hitler, load their tank with 7.5cm ammunition. Officially the tank had internal racks for 87 rounds, but many crews managed to load more.

PzKpfw IV Production 1944

	Accepted by Waffenamt	Actual stock	PzKpfw IV (kurz)	PzKpfw IV (lang)
January	300	1,668	176	1,492
February	252	1,710	167	1,543
March	310	1,821	164	1,657
April	299	2,159	163	1,996
May	302	2,119	164	1,955
June	300	2,304	166	2,138
July	300	2,336	159	2,177
August	300	2,128	161	1,967
September	180	2,101	159	1,942
October	212	1,620	161	1,459 °
November	225	1,620	95 °	1,525
December	195	1,710	80	1,630
January 45	170	1,684	80	1,604
February 45	160	1,571	80	1,491
March 45	55	?	?	?
April 45	?	?	?	?

° Stocks corrected

Intentionally or not, Guderian's statements did not quite correspond to reality (in September 1943 assault guns were equipped with a machine gun, and the front armour on the PzKpfw IV had been also increased to 80mm). However, he won the argument and the PzKpfw IV remained in production.

Ironically, in this situation a bombing raid on the Alkett factory hit *Sturmgeschütz* production hard. In order to compensate for the missing assault guns Krupp was instructed to terminate production of the PzKpfw IV and to mount the assault gun's superstructure onto the hull of the PzKpfw IV.

Only three months later the production of the StuG IV began. These vehicles were to be deployed almost exclusively to the tank destroyer units of infantry and *Volksgrenadier* divisions at a rate of ten or fourteen in each company.

The 1944 production figures submitted by the *Waffenamt* again show a number of discrepancies. In October and November, the records were corrected for unknown reasons. From December 1944 to February 1945 the stock of 7.5cm KwK L/24 armed PzKpfw IV is given as 80, indicating that these vehicles were possibly deployed with training and replacement units only.

The statistics also shows losses. For instance, during September 1944 some 771 PzKpfw IV lang were recorded as lost in combat, the highest monthly number during the war.

Technical Progress

After all attempts to improve the PzKpfw IV radically had to be abandoned, the tank remained in production. After the conversion of production at Krupp, two companies remained in the program, VOMAG and Nibelungenwerk. The products of both companies were almost identical. In February 1944 production of the PzKpfw IV Ausf J, or 10.BW, began. Until the end of the war, more than 3,000 of this model were to be built.

In the course of further production, only simplifications were introduced. A new type of widened *Winterketten* (winter tracks) had been introduced by late 1943. The new tracks called *Ostketten* (east tracks) were far more substantial, being similar to the tracks of the Tiger tank. Unlike the former, the *Ostkette* links did not tend to break.

The electrical turret drive, together with the associated power generator, was taken out of production. The manually operated drive was equipped with a second reduction gear to facilitate rotation when the vehicle was in an inclined position. This modification was regularly described as disadvantageous in various reports. The visors and pistol ports in the turret side hatches were dropped.

In September the steel plate type *Panzerschürzen* were replaced by cheaper wire mesh. One of the few improvements was the strengthening of the superstructure and turret roof armour and the installation of a close

Above: In October 1944, the Nibelungenwerke factory was hit by Allied bombers. A number of completed tanks were badly damaged including these PzKpfw IV Ausf J. All have the mounting rail for the wire mesh-type *Panzerschürzen* and are painted in *Licht-und-Schatten Tarnung* (light and shadow) ambush camouflage.

Right: The bomb blast has torn-off the last segment of mesh-type *Panzerschürzen*. Note the horizontal exhaust silencer (muffler) has been replaced by *Flammenvernichter* (flame suppressor) pipes.

defense weapon in the turret. In September the application of *Zimmerit* was cancelled.

In June 1944, VOMAG in Plauen was to stop production of the PzKpfw IV in favour of the new type of assault gun (*Jagdpanzer* IV). Thus, contrary to Guderian's ideas, a significant part of PzKpfw IV production was to be converted to *Sturmgeschütz* (now called *Jagdpanzer*).

Command Tank

The *Funkgerät* (Fu – radio device) was obligatory for all German tanks. Basically, this equipment consisted of a 10W VHF transmitter and two receivers:

- One Fu 5 radio installation: VHF 10W Sender (S – transmitter) 'e' and a VHF *Empfänger* (E – receiver) 'e' plus converters.
- One Fu 2 consisting of an *Empfänger* 'e' and converters.

The transmitter allowed a range of 2km (voice) or up to 4km (morse). Both radios relied on a 2m rod antenna.

In the first half of the war most tanks in the company were only equipped with Fu 2, only the tanks of platoon and company commanders were fitted with the additional Fu 5. Later, the combination of Fu 5 and Fu 2 seems to have become standard.

At staff level in tank divisions, regiments, infantry and signal units all were assigned a *Panzerbefehlswagen* (PzBeflWg – command tank) equipped with a Fu 5 radio with an additional long-range radio:

- A Fu 8 radio set consisting of a 30W S MW/AM transmitter and Fu 4 MW/AM E 'c' receiver plus converters which had a voice range of up to 40km; 120km (Morse) mode. Initially, a large frame-type antenna

PzKpfw IV Ausf J

Weight:	25,401kg
Engine:	Maybach HL120 TRM
Performance:	265hp
Speed (maximum):	38kph
Range (road):	210km
Range (cross country):	130km
Trench crossing:	2.3m
Fording depth:	80cm
Ground clearance:	40cm

The first *grosser Panzerbefehlswagen* (PzBefWg – large command tank) was a planned development of the PzKpfw III, whereas a similar command tank based on the PzKpfw IV was not produced until March 1944. Here a PzKpfw IV Ausf F – the last *Ausführung* (model/mark) to mount the 7.5cm KwK L/24 – in service with 13.PzDiv, has been modified in the field and fitted with a frame antenna taken from a PzBefWg III.

was mounted over the engine deck: in 1942, a far less conspicuous *Sternantenne* (star antenna) 'd' was fitted. PzBefWg with this equipment received the designation SdKfz 268.

– Alternatively, for air-to-ground communications the Fu 7, a MW/AM 30W S and a E 'c', was supplied. The equipment had a voice range of 100km when fitted with a 1.4m rod antenna.

– Command tanks with this equipment were designated *Sonderkraftfahrzeug* (SdKfz – special purpose vehicle) 267.

In principle, all German tank types could be delivered with this extended radio equipment, including the PzKpfw 35(t) and PzKpfw 38(t) and PzKpfw III. In the years preceding the war the decision had already been made to introduce a relatively large number of command tanks based on the PzKpfw III. Since these vehicles were deployed some distance from the front, some remained in action until the end of the war. While the first command tanks were special constructions, from 1943 on the radio equipment was designed in such a way

that a retrofit in normal tanks in the field was possible without problems. This also led to a simplification of production. Thanks to the use of a star antenna, these PzBefWg basing on PzKpfw IV, PzKpfw V Panther and PzKpfw VI Tiger could hardly be distinguished from normal tanks. The main ordnance remained fully operational, a further advantage.

Command tanks based on the PzKpfw IV were not available until the end of 1943 (except for troop conversions).

Panzerbeobachtungswagen IV

With the introduction of the self-propelled artillery – *Wespe* (wasp) and *Hummel* (bumble bee) – the introduction of specialized armoured artillery observation vehicles was demanded. These vehicles were to be assigned to the artillery observers to follow the tank assault. The vehicles were externally similar to standard battle tanks, having comparable armour protection. Between February 1943 and April 1944, some 262 *Panzerbeobachtungswagen* (PzBeobWg – artillery observation tanks) were built using refurbished PzKpfw III chassis. These vehicles had:

- A Fu 8 radio set consisting of a 30W S MW/AM transmitter and a MW/AM E 'c' receiver plus converter, as used by the command tanks to contact the Panzer regiment.
- A FuSprechGer 'f' for communication with the battery officer of the artillery unit.
- A portable TonFuGer 'g' when the forward observer had to leave his tank.

A PzKpfw IV Ausf G originally produced in May 1943, was returned to Germany for a major general overhaul but was converted into a command tank and returned to service in early 1944. A 2m rod-type aerial for the standard *Funkgerät* (Fu – radio device) 5 is mounted on the turret roof; a 1.4m *Sternantenne* (star antenna) 'd' for the long-range Fu 8 could be mounted in place of the standard aerial. The 2m rod-type aerial mounted at the rear is for Fu 7 ground-to-air communication.

A PzKpfw IV Ausf G, mounting a 7.5cm KwK 40 L/48 gun, is in service with the staff company on an unknown PzAbt. The *Turmsfernrohr* (TSR – commander's periscope) is visible next to the open hatch.

Mounts for artillery observation equipment such as a *Scherenfernrohr* (SF – scissors periscope) and an *Turmbeobachtungsfernrohr* (TBF – turret observation periscope) 2 and a *Turmsfernrohr* (TSR – commander's periscope) were added in the turret of the PzBeobWg III. The tank mounted a dummy gun.

As these vehicles often failed in combat due to their age, they were not welcomed. From January 1944, new-production PzKpfw IV were converted to create a more efficient PzBeobWg. Externally they were almost identical to standard PzKpfw IV. However, instead of the conventional PzKpfw IV commander's cupola the much flatter cupola of the *Sturmgeschütz* was installed.

PzKpfw IV Debate

In August 1944, Guderian again had to fight for the PzKpfw IV. Production of the PzKpfw III had been cancelled in August 1943 and had almost completely stopped – with the important exception of the chassis being built for the StuG III. In view of the tense tank situation in his tank divisions, Guderian fought all demands to transfer the PzKpfw IV production to assault guns. During a *Führerbesprechung* (lecture to the Führer) he repeated his position once again:

PzKpfw IV, weaponry and tactical deployment:

The 7.5cm KwK L/48 with PzGrPatr 39 is sufficient to combat all British, American and Russian tank types encountered so far at the average battle ranges of 8,000m to 12,000m (including PzKpfw Cromwell). Experience reports on the use of the PzKpfw IV in comparison with assault guns deployed in Sicily, Italy and Normandy, all agree that the assault gun is inferior to the PzKpfw with rotating turret.

PzKpfw IV, technical:

The PzKpfw IV is currently our most mature tank design in which every tanker has full confidence. The *Sturmgeschütz* on PzKpfw IV chassis must be considered as an emergency solution, which is considered to be inferior to the *Sturmgeschütz* on chassis III [StuG III].
The final drive is the weak point of the PzKpfw IV chassis, and since the assault gun must aim at targets by turning the complete vehicle, there is a continuously higher

The end of the war for a German tank crew: A PzKfw IV Ausf J passes a group of US soldiers on the way to a collection compound for captured vehicles.

load on both the brakes and the final drive. The gears in the drive reduction therefore broke in increasing numbers, and therefore represent a considerable bottleneck in production and spare parts supply.

Final Judgement

All available troop experiences submitted by tank units speak clearly in favour of the tank with rotating turret, over the *Sturmgeschütz*. All enemy tanks and assault gun types that have appeared so far are destroyed with our current armour-piercing weapons, including the 7.5cm KwK L/48.

Changing the production of PzKpfw IV to *Sturmgeschütz* would mean that the supply for the existing PzKpfw IV units would consist of assault guns to ensure battlefield readiness. This would mean that within these units two different tank types, whose operational principles are fundamentally different, would have to be combined.

Two US Army infantrymen observe a raid by Allied ground-attack aircraft from the cover provided by a knocked-out PzKpfw IV Ausf J. Any movement by German armour over open terrain was fraught with danger.

By this time the new British Cruiser Tank Mk VIII Cromwell was encountered on the Western Front. This interesting design was possibly overestimated by the German authorities. In the report, the large-scale introduction of the Josef Stalin (JS) II is reported almost incidentally. The type was fitted with a 122mm cannon almost twice as powerful as the 7.5cm KwK L/48, making it a most dangerous opponent for the PzKpfw IV.

In November 1944, the fate of the PzKpfw IV was again under discussion. On 8 November 1944, a decision was made at a *Führerbesprechung*:

> Production of the [PzKpfw IV] tank is to be discontinued in favour of the PzKpfw 38(t) and the PzKpfw V Panther. This will result in a further reduction of types and a simplification of the supply of spare parts. After conversion to the PzKpfw 38(t), this vehicle will be used for:
> – *Sturmgeschütz*
> – Reconnaissance tank

– Artillery observation vehicle

– Flak-Panzer AA gun tank

– Weapon carrier for le Fh, s Fh, 8.8cm PaK, 12.8cm PaK and 15cm sIG

The assault tank (15cm) will continue to be built on PzKpfw IV chassis transferred from factory overhauling vehicles.

In this context the term *Sturmgeschütz* is analogous to *Panzerjäger* (tank destroyer). The PzKpfW IV would however remain in production.

In May 1944, PzRgt 39 (17.PzDiv) reported serious quality problems:

On 17 April, 1944, seventeen new PzKpfw IV Ausf J were assigned to the division and taken over by a delivery command in Linz an der Donau. A detailed technical inspection of the PzKpfw by the delivery team did not take place. On 19 April 1944, these PzKpfw were unloaded in Halicz and transferred to the operation area after a land march of some 60km. After only a few hundred metres of driving PzKpfw [chassis number] 89861, broke down due to damage to the brakes (breakage of the fibre coupling and sheared brake-pad studs). After about 30km, tank No.89939 broke down with gearbox, brake and final drive damage. It was immediately transported to the K-Werk Süd in Sanok.

The tanks Nos.89941/932/836/934/913/920 also broke down during the march, but were able to continue their journey after repair. Strangely enough, almost all PzKpfw had brake damage on the left brakes only.

After four years of occupation, German tanks, here a PzKpfw IV Ausf J with the tactical number '214', were often confronted by hostile crowds in French or Belgium cities, particularly after Allied forces began advancing out of Normandy. This serves as a show of force.

All tanks arriving at the department were subjected to a detailed mechanical inspection by the workshop team and all required basic adjustments to be made to the brakes.

Brake bands have been poorly adjusted, many are incorrectly installed, retaining screws are misaligned and unevenly tightened; many of the locking nuts had not been tightened. Brake drums are not sufficiently tightened. The clearance between the brake drum and brake band appears to be incorrectly adjusted.

In addition, the following damage or defects have also been found:

The left-hand reduction gear on No.89934 had a fastening nut on the large spur gear left unsecured. As a result, the nut loosened and caused a cog to fracture. While installing a new final drive, further nuts were found to be loose.

Tank Nos.89940/617/556/876/ and No.90018 failed after only a short period of use with transmission damage. The cause was almost always the third gear. In the case of tank No.89941, the bolts retaining the fuel pump loosened.

Considering the damage, it seems that apparently no test runs had taken place in the factory. The brakes had not yet been correctly bedded-in, and the brake system had not been finally adjusted. Driving with badly adjusted brakes or an incorrectly

In June 1944, 2.SS-PzDiv Das Reich was stationed in the south of France in anticipation of an Allied landing. Here four PzKpfw IV from the division take part in one of the many preparatory exercises.

Normandy 1944: What appears to be a virtually undamaged PzKpfw IV Ausf G being towed by a Centaur ARV (armoured recovery vehicle) of a British Army engineer unit.

The crew of a PzKpfw IV Ausf H: The commander, a young-looking *Leutnant*, wears a 'splinter camouflage'-type overall, while his men have standard issue black uniforms.

installed brake system naturally resulted in damage due to excess strain and significant wear. The air baffle plates, which used to be on the brake drums, are missing on the J series, which results in an undesirable increase in temperature.

Some of the problems affecting the PzKpfw IV were attributed to poor workmanship at Nibelungenwerk.

Difficult terrain sometimes required the use of small tank combat squads as reported in the October 1944 issue of the *Nachrichtenblatt der Panzertruppe*:

> The peculiarity of the deeply undulating terrain and the weakness of our tank force made any counterattack impossible. Any crossing of the heights would have eliminated the element of surprise and also our tanks would have been easily knocked out by enemy tanks or by the numerous anti-tank guns positioned in their frontline. Consequently, we fired on the enemy from elevated positions. Our tanks were completely dug-in some 100m to 200m away from where our tank destroyers were positioned. Observation posts would provide early warning of any enemy attack.

The enemy used its tanks in this combat section only for local counterattacks in groups of up to six tanks. The combat efficiency of the Sherman tanks with Russian crews does not seem to be very high, because the Soviet tank man has little confidence in this type. Crews often abandoned their tanks after the first rounds hit. The Sherman, like the T-34, is vulnerable to the superior firepower of the PzKpfw IV or a similarly armed StuG.

In general, the firefight was conducted at distances between 1,200m and 2,200m. After tanks and tank destroyers had opened fire, our artillery continued to support, although they rarely hit an individual tank. The thick cloud of dust and smoke caused by the artillery fire allowed the enemy tanks to retreat back over the edge of the mountain.

It is important that our forward observers immediately order our artillery to cease fire as soon as our own tanks and tank destroyers take up the fight against enemy tanks.

A senior officer added the following comment:

This way of fighting is only to be employed if the terrain forces it. An agile fighting style using numerous alternative positions and immediate retreat into full cover is necessary.

Two German tank crewmen inspect the effect their 7.5cm KwK 40 gun has had on the front armour of a US Army M4A3 Sherman.

Above: A PzKpfw IV Ausf J fitted with wire-mesh side skirts, which were also known as '*Thoma schilde*'. The type gave the same level of protection as early mild steel *Panzerschürzen* but were cheaper to produce and less heavy.

Right: This PzKpfw IV Ausf J was possibly hit by air-to-ground rockets fired by an Allied fighter-bomber aircraft which ignited the fuel causing the ammunition stowed inside the tank to explode.

After D-Day: 6 June 1944

The September 1944 issue of *Nachrichtblatt der Panzertruppe* contains extracts from the interrogation of a captured British officer:

> The British infantry has special difficulties with the excellently camouflaged German machine-gun nests and snipers in trees. The German tanks are usually so well camouflaged that they are only discovered by the infantry when it is too late. The PIAT [Projector, Infantry, Anti-Tank] has little effect against a German tank, since they have sheet metal protection [*Panzerschürzen*] on the side, which makes the grenades explode before they even reach the actual tank.

This report shows that the side skirts as used with the PzKpfw IV were also effective against modern anti-tank weapons. The British PIAT, although inferior in performance to the *Faustpatrone* or the *Panzerschreck*, was an effective weapon, which could penetrate 80mm frontal armour at less than 100m range.

On the western front, the M4 Sherman would become the most important tank type. Besides the US Army, Canadian, British, French and Polish tank forces were equipped with this versatile vehicle. The tank was designed to be mass produced and was better armoured than the PzKpfw IV, especially at the side and rear. The German 7.5cm KwK 40 was clearly superior to Shermans which mounted a 75mm gun. With the introduction of the 76mm M1 gun the situation would change and gave the Sherman a clear superiority. The British Firefly mounted a powerful Ordnance Quick Firing 17-pounder quick firing gun, which had similar performance.

The *General der Panzertruppe* analysed the tanks and fighting style of the Western Allies several times. An article in *Nachrichtenblat der Panzertruppe*, published in February 1945, reported:

> Compilation of experiences in the West
>
> The effective combat range of our own and enemy tanks depends on the firing position and especially on the position of the tanks to each other: It makes a big difference whether the battle is fought front-to-front or front-to-side. On the basis of experience the following can be said:
> The PzKpfw IV penetrates the Sherman at distances below 1,000m, but will be penetrated by the Sherman up to 2,000m if the angle of impact is favourable. Panther and Tiger are far superior.
>
> Enemy tank combat style

The Americans and the British always attempt to avoid open and mobile tank-versus-tank combat, because they mistrust the ability of the leadership as well as the range of the tank guns. Tank attacks are only conducted if they can be supported by ample artillery and air force deployment. He tries to draw out the fire of our own tanks at an early stage in order to destroy them with the combined fire of his artillery and air force.

Italy 1944: The commander of a PzKpfw IV Ausf J from 2.SS-PzDiv Das Reich observes the battlefront from a lightly camouflaged position.

Defence against enemy tanks

The enemy has to be forced to retreat by our tank and anti-tank reserves. These are placed at the focal point of an enemy tank attack, and will fire at his flanks in such a way that the enemy can be defeated when confronted by our own tanks.

Here a change in German tank tactics is obvious, and had already been tried on the Russian battlefront. The weakened combat strength of German tank divisions did not allow offensive operations, either limited or far-reaching.

In France, German forces had to deal with an opponent who, in addition to having material superiority, was also similarly strong in tactical leadership, and Allied air superiority prevented the Germans from deploying larger tank formations.

Soviet Union

On the Russian side, series production of the T-34/85 began in 1944. The medium tank was now equipped with a new, more heavily armoured turret and carried an 85mm gun. This tank was far superior to the PzKpfw IV.

A PzKpfw IV Ausf H on a *Sonderanhänger* (SdAnh – special purpose trailer) 116 is carefully manoeuvered around a tight curve; a regular problem faced by German recovery teams in the difficult terrain of Italy.

The *Bocage* country in Normandy – sunken lanes protected by banks topped with tall thick hedgerow – was not ideal for tank-versus-tank warfare. Here British infantry run past a knocked-out PzKpfw IV Ausf G as Allied forces begin to advance from the D-Day beaches. (Getty)

The heavy tank KV would evolve into the Josef Stalin (JS) -II. The type was extremely heavily armoured, and could only be penetrated by the 7.5cm KwK 40 L/48 under advantageous circumstances. The JS-II was armed with a formidable 122mm cannon.

While PzKpfw V Panther and both PzKpfw VI Tiger Ausf E and the later Tiger II Ausf B could deal with these new adversaries, units issued with PzKpfw IV and *Sturmgeschütz* had to develop and apply sophisticated tactics. One was known as the '*Feuersack*' (fire sack): a single or a pair of JS-II heavy tanks would be lured into a trap where two hidden PzKpfw IV were lined up on each side. When the enemy tanks attacked their 'target', they would be fired on from the flanks at the closest possible range. This procedure often proved successful, but was only possible in confusing terrain. A direct confrontation with a JS-II was unpromising and hazardous.

Officers of 12.SS-PzDiv Hitlerjugend inspect a PzKpfw IV during a training exercise. Note the double set of towing cables and the small exhaust for the petrol-powered DKW auxiliary generator which supplied electric current to the turret traversing motor.

A PzKpfw IV Ausf H from PzRgt 35 (4.PzDiv). The crew has fitted an interesting collection of tracks – PzKfw IV, PzKpfw V Panther and an Allied M3 Grant – to it for extra protection.

In January 1945, the *Generalinspekteur der Panzertruppe* published a note which, in a way, documented the general helplessness felt by his troops:

Loyalty to the tank

On 6 October of this year [1944] the PzKpfw IV of driver *Gefreiter* Schattenkirchner of the PzRgt 35 was loaded onto a train to be transported to the workshop. During the ride the train suddenly stopped, because the enemy had already reached and captured the railway line. When the order to blow up the tank was given, Schattenkirchner boarded the tank, made a turn and drove the tank off. Despite damage to the final drive, he was able to continue for another 8km before arranging for it to be recovered by a heavy half-track tractor. The Inspector General of the Tank Corps expresses his special appreciation to Schattenkirchner for his unparalleled performance in the line of duty and dedication to saving the tank entrusted to him.

Above: A squad of grenadiers, armed with 7.92mm *Karibiner* 98k and *Maschinenpistole* (MP – machine pistol) 40, hitch a ride crowded on the engine cover of a PzKpfw IV Ausf H. The improved mounting brackets for the *Panzerschürzen* are clearly visible.

Right: A column of PzKpfw IV during the retreat from Bastogne, Belgium, in January 1945.

Left: The crew of a PzKfpw IV from 2.Kp, I.Abt/PzRgt 35 replenish the ammunition ready for the next battle. The *Oberfeldwebel* (left) has been awarded two *Panzervernichtungs- abzeichen* (tank destruction badges) for the destruction of an enemy tank in close combat.

Below: A PzKpfw IV Ausf H: During production of this model, the front section of the turret roof was reinforced from 10mm to 16mm, and the section around the cupola was increased to 25mm.

Above: Two PzKpfw IV Ausf J from PzRgt 33 (9.PzDiv) loaded on an SSys railway wagon. Known as the 'Vienna division', the unit used the distinctive Prinz Eugen badge (a mounted knight).

Right: A PzKpfw IV Ausf H of PzRgt 8 (10.PzDiv): the crew has placed extra fuel cans on the turret in preparation for a long transfer march.

Left: The chassis No.89589 identifies this PzKpfw IV Ausf J, as one of those manufactured at the Nibelingenwerke. The tank is in service with 2.PzDiv; note the Trident symbol used by the division from 1943.

Below: Only a few units used four-digit turret numbers which identifies this as a PzKpfw IV Ausf J of III.Abt/PzRgt 24, from 12.*Schwadron* (squadron).

A late production PzKpfw IV Ausf J: Note the extended towing eyes and that there are no ventilation domes on the brake maintenance hatches.

Towards the end of the war, the supply situation on the frontlines was inevitably to worsen. It was still possible to make extraordinary efforts with the last resources available – examples are the Battle of the Bulge and *Unternehmen Konrad II*, the defence of Budapest. But the individual armoured divisions were only a shadow of their former might.

Comparative Tanks in 1945

Type	PzKpfw IV Ausf J	T-34/76	M4 Medium	PzKpfw V Panther
Ordnance:	7.5cm KwK 40 L/48 Two MG 34	76.2cm L/41 F-34 Two MG	75mm L/31 M1 Three MG	7.5cm KwK L/70 Two MG 34
Performance:	265hp	500hp	400hp	700hp
Weight:	25,000kg	26,300kg	30,400kg	46,000kg
Ground clearance:	40cm	38cm	43cm	56cm
Speed (maximum):	38kph	47kph	40.2kph	55kph
Range (road):	320km	455km	193km	200km
Range (cross country):	210km	260km	no info	100km

The 11.PzDiv can be taken as an example. The unit, when attached to *Heeresgruppe* B, was engaged in the defensive battles around Trier, almost in the middle of the Reich. In 1944, the division was successfully restructured according to the Panzer Division 44 structure, and in accordance the division was entitled to the following strength: 81 PzKpfw IV, ten ready for action;

When the Josef Stalin (JS) II entered service, the Red Army had a heavy tank able to defeat with a PzKpfw VI Tiger Ausf E. The 122mm D-25T gun could easily destroy a PzKpfw IV Ausf H at long range, which required commanders to adopt ambush tactics.

M4A3 (76) HVSS	T-34/85	PzKpfw VI Ausf B	JS-II	M26 heavy tank
76mm	85mm L/53	8.8cm	122mm	90mm
L/52 M1	SiS S-53	KwK 43 L/71	L/45 D-25 T	L/53 M3
Three MG	Two MG	Two MG 34	Two MG	Three MG
500hp	500hp	700hp	520hp	500hp
33,700kg	30,000kg	69,800kg	46,000kg	41,800kg
43cm	45cm	49cm	42cm	no info
40.8kph	47kph	41.5kph	32kph	40kph
161km	300km	170 km	240km	161km
no info	160km	120km	210km	no info

An immobilized PzKpfw IV from PzRgt 29 (12. PzDiv) about to be towed to a Workstatt (workshop) by an SdKfz 9 *schwerer Zugkraftwagen* (heavy half-track tractor).

79 PzKpfw V Panthers of which 32 were combat ready; the PzGrenAbt was equipped with 57 light and medium armoured half-track vehicles and the PzJgAbt still had seven of the 31 StuG IV ready for action. The commander of 11.PzDiv lists several complaints:

a) Level of training: The few battle-hardened men of the PzGrenAbt were killed or wounded in the last heavy fighting. The training level of the available replacements is completely insufficient. In the field replacement battalion for the division there are corresponding training courses for recruits and replacement tank crews.

b) Degree of mobility: The division is 80 percent mobile.

c) Mood of the troops: Many of the division come from eastern Germany and are disturbed by the Soviet offensive. The absence of mail, worries about relatives and a ban on leave create a very desolate mood. But, in general their attitude is nevertheless satisfactory.

d) Possible deployment: An offensive deployment of the division is not possible

at the time due to the severe losses suffered by our PzGren.

e) Combat value: The division is suitable only for defence

f) Special difficulties:
Personnel: Grenadier elements of the division need to be reinforced
Material: Division is equipped with a large number of foreign-produced light motor vehicles. Due to spare parts problems, the stock of operational vehicles is only small. The fuel situation does not allow for the regular maintenance of the operational armoured vehicles, and the resulting damage will not become apparent until the next operation. The lack of all-terrain passenger cars, medium and heavy trucks is particularly noticeable in the current area of operation and is exacerbated by the prevailing weather conditions.

In the final months of the war, a number of German cities were declared to be a fortress. Here the turret from a PzKpfw IV Ausf J has been dug into the ground to serve as a pillbox. The reinforced roof of the turret is visible, but the cupola has been removed.

Right: A British Army M4A2 DD (Duplex Drive) swimming tank, passes a knocked-out PzKpfw IV Ausf H as Allied forces advance along a country lane in Normandy.

Below: A US Army M4A3 Sherman: It was common practice to pack sandbags around the superstructure and turret for extra protection against German *Panzerfaust* (tank fist) and *Panzerschreck* (tank shock) close combat anti-tank weapons.

Left: Officers of PzRgt 35 (4.PzDiv) salute a superior officer travelling in an SdKfz 251/6 *Kommandowagen* (command vehicle).

Below: The US continued to deliver tanks under the Lend-Lease Program to the Soviet Union until late 1944. These included the M4A3 Sherman armed with a 76mm M1A1 high-velocity gun, which was sufficiently powerful to defeat a PzKpfw V Panther and PzKpfw VI Tiger Ausf E.

Tanks played a vital role on virtually every battlefront in World War II. The long-serving German PzKpfw IV was an outstanding tank until up-gunned variants of the Soviet T-34 (also the KV-85 and JS-2) and the US-built M4 Sherman entered service. Although originally planned as an escort tank, the type had already, despite being classified as a support weapon, proven to be very effective against better armoured enemy tanks. Its simple basic design allowed the type to be easily modified to meet battlefield conditions by improving armament and armour protection for a crew.

The sudden appearance of the Soviet-built T-34, in the first few months of *Unternehmen* Barbarossa, caused problems for the crews of PzKpfw IV until shaped-charge ammunition became available for the 7.5cm KwK L/24 gun. In 1942, the *Langrohr* (lang – long-barrel) 7.5cm KwK L/43 tank gun was mounted in the PzKpfw IV Ausf F. An improved 7.5cm KwK L/48 was introduced when the PzKpfw IV Ausf H to Ausf K entered service.

Between 1942 and 1943, the PzKpfw IV was numerically the most important tank in the German arsenal.

In April 1943, the commander of 17.PzDiv, *Generalleutnant* Fridolin von Senger und Etterlin, submitted a report to the headquarters of LVIII.PzKorps:

Statement:
During our *Blitzkrieg* attacks, firstly on Poland in 1939 and then the Low Countries and France in 1940, the large-scale deployment and tactics employed by our Panzer divisions proved to be decisive. This allowed our infantry and other supporting elements to capture and hold large areas of enemy territory.

But the tactics that led to the great successes in 1939, 1940 and the first part of Barbarossa in 1941 must now be considered as outdated. Even if it is still possible

An *Automitrailleuse de Reconnaissance* Renault *Modele* 1933 (AMR 33) light cavalry tank begins to burn after being hit by a 7.5cm round fired by one of these PzKpfw IV Ausf B from 1.PzDiv.

1938: Tanks of PzRgt 1 (1.PzDiv) parade through the grounds of their home garrison in Erfurt in Thuringia. The regiment had a mixed complement of PzKpfw IV Ausf A and Ausf B or Ausf C.

today to smash through anti-tank defences by attacking in several waves, we can no longer afford this procedure, since it always results in considerable losses. This in turn leads to a rapid, and virtually unstoppable, depletion of our tank reserves to the point where the effectiveness of a Panzer division will deteriorate dramatically. A change in tactics is the only logical course of action. The initial success of any new weapon is based on the enemy being unable to neutralize its initial effect, but he will soon adapt or develop an appropriate defence.

From a supply point of view, tank production cannot keep pace with our requirements for new or replacement tanks.

Von Senger und Etterlin – his son Ferdinand was recruited into the German *Bundeswehr* [armed forces] after the war – spoke with an insight that is hardly surprising in 1943. Consistent reports from other tank and assault gun units came to similar conclusions.

The division commander demanded tank tactics should be fundamentally changed:

> The *Panzergruppe* no longer forms the core of the tank division, it must now be considered as an integral part of an army group and operate in conjunction with all other units. The tank is not a new weapon, but when it is deployed in combination with others, it still has its significance even if the number of tanks has fallen far below the intended target. Its significance lies in the fact that it combines mobility and firepower, which are important for an attack. But it must be remembered that the tank is all too often vulnerable when the enemy deploys a more powerful anti-tank weapon that can defeat our armour.

In fact, his ideas almost suggest that the tank force should be downgraded, when at that time the military was investing a vast amount of time, money and other resources in developing the PzKpfw VI Tiger Ausf E heavy tank and the PzKpfw V Panther medium tank.

From 1944 onwards, although mechanically reliable, the PzKpfw IV fell behind in terms of performance, but could still be deployed to great effect especially when commanded by a well-trained officer and manned with an experienced crew. German forces, especially those on the Eastern Front, always proved flexible and able to adapt their tactics as a battle developed.

From 1943, the Red Army adopted new tactics and went from the desperate defence of their country to launching a two-year offensive which would take them to Berlin in May 1945.

In the West, the D-Day landings on the beaches of Normandy by Allied forces on 6 June 1944 was a decisive blow. The under-equipped, under-manned and battle-weary German armed forces were now fighting on two fronts to save the Fatherland.

Both Allied and Soviet forces seemed to have an inexhaustible supply of manpower, an endless supply of replacement equipment and, eventually, control of the skies over the battlefront. Faced by such adversaries, the German Reich would ultimately fall.

However, what did remain of the Panzer divisions fought hard until the war ended – the PzKpfw IV was still in the vanguard.

1938: Tanks of PzRgt 1 (1.PzDiv) parade through the grounds of their home garrison in Erfurt in Thuringia. The regiment had a mixed complement of PzKpfw IV Ausf A and Ausf B or Ausf C.

The railway yard at
the Nibelungenwerk in
February 1943: A number
of PzKpfw IV Ausf G,
finished in *Dunkelgelb*
(dark yellow), have been
loaded on *Deutsche
Reichsbahn* (German State
Railways) standard flat-
bed wagons for delivery to
a distribution depot.

Support Vehicles

In 1943, Altmarkische Kettenwerke (Alkett) was contracted to develop a *Selbstfahrlafette* (Sfl – self-propelled) gun carriage by utilizing standard chassis components from the PzKpfw III and PzKpfw IV. The result was the *Geschützwagen* (GW – gun carrier) III/IV which was used as the chassis for the heavy tank destroyer SdKfz 164 *Hornisse* (hornet) – later *Nashorn* (rhinoceros): (*Panzerjäger: Volume 2*, Osprey 2020) and also the 15cm *Panzerhaubitze* 18 auf GW III/IV *Hummel* (bumble bee) self-propelled howitzer, SdKfz 165. (*Panzerartillerie*: Osprey 2019).

Spring 1944 saw the *Nashorn* tank destroyer beginning to be replaced by a 'revolutionary new assault gun', the *Jagdpanzer* (hunting tank) IV, which entered service at the same time as the *Jagdpanzer* 38(t) *Hetzer* (baiter). Both vehicles – the Hetzer was originally armed with a 7.5cm PaK 39 L/48 – mounted the 7.5cm KwK L/48 as used in the PzKpfw IV Ausf H.

Parallel to this, some 1,000 *Sturmgeschütz* IV armed with the 7.5cm *Sturmkanone* (StuK – assault gun) 49 L/48 were to be produced by the end of the war.

In 1944, in order to give the tank destroyer urgently needed more effective firepower, the 7.5cm KwK 42 L/70 high-power cannon was installed in the *Jagdpanzer* IV.

From 1943, the GW III/IV was also used as the chassis for three types of *Flugzeugabwehrkanone-Panzer* (FlaK-Pz – anti-aircraft tank) which were to equip *Flugzeugabwehrkanone-Zug* (FlaK-Zg – anti-aircraft platoons). The first mounted a 3.7cm FlaK 43 L/60 protected by four hinged armoured panels which could be folded down: it was known as the *Möbelwagen* (furniture van) and a total of 240 were built. The second known as *Wirbelwind* (whirlwind), was armed with four 2cm FlaK 38 L/55, in a quadruple mounting, inside an open-top rotatable turret. Approximately 100 were built on refurbished PzKpfw IV by Ostbau Werke located at *Ersatz und Ausbildungs Abteilung* (replacement and training battalion) 15 in Sagan, Silesia. The third was known as the *Ostwind* (east wind), and mounted a 3.7cm FlaK 43 L/60 in a hexagonal-shaped rotatable turret, which was also built at Ostbau Werke. A total of 44 were completed of which seven were new-build vehicles, the remaining 37 being built on refurbished PzKpw IV.

Another specialized variant was developed in 1943, the *Sturmpanzer IV* – known as *Brummbär* (grizzly bear) – mounting a 15cm *Sturmhaubitz* (StuH – assault howitzer) 43 L/12 in a heavily armoured superstructure, designed to assist German units in urban warfare.

The PzKpfw IV was delivered to a number of German allies, including Bulgaria, Finland, Romania and Spain. Turkey also acquired a small number.

The Soviet Union used a significant number of captured PzKpfw IV to equip front-line units and later used the type for training tank crews.

After the war various countries supplied a large number of PzKpfw IV to Syria, but most were lost in 1967 during 'The Six-Day War' with Israel.

The bottomless mud on the Eastern Front has halted a PzKpfw IV Ausf H from 5.SS-PzDiv Wiking and also a *Maultier* (mule) half-track truck.

US Army infantry armed with the Bazooka – a man-portable recoilless anti-tank rocket launcher – inspect a damaged PzKpfw IV after the D-Day landings on 6 June 1944. (Getty)

INDEX

Acknowledgements

As with my previous books, I have searched and gathered much original information from a number of public archives, including the Bundesarchiv/Militärarchiv in Freiburg, Germany, and the National Archives & Records Administration, Washington, USA. Furthermore, the internet-based Project for the Digitizing of German Documents in Archives of the Russian Federation was used to a great extent.

Only a few post-war publications have been used for reference when writing this book. However, *Panzertracts* written and edited by Thomas Jentz, is much valued since they contain accurate information. Also, I commend those publications written by Walter J. Spielberger.

I also want to acknowledge my appreciation to Peter Müller (Historyfacts) for supplying me with much vital information and advice.

Many thanks to those individuals who have provided assistance and also access to their archives and collections of other material:

Florian von Aufseß, Sergei Netrebenko, Peter Müller (Historyfacts), Jürgen Wilhelm, Wolfgang Schneider, Karlheinz Münch, Henry Hoppe, Markus Zöllner and Holger Erdmann.

Finally, my sincere thanks to my editor Jasper Spencer-Smith, an ever-patient gentleman, and also to Nigel Pell for his, as always, excellent page layout.

Unless otherwise indicated, all images in this book are from the Thomas Anderson Collection.

Bibliography

Panzertruppen Volume 1 and Volume 2, Thomas Jentz, Podzun-Pallas
Panzertracts, several volumes, *Panzertracts*, Maryland, USA
Begleitwagen Panzerkapmfwagen IV, Walter J. Spielberger. Motorbuch Verlag
Verbände und Truppen der deutschen Wehrmacht, 16 Volumes, G. Tessin